HAWAIIAN SHIRTS
Dress Right for Paradise

Nancy N. Schiffer

Schiffer Publishing Ltd.
4880 Lower Valley Road, Atglen, PA 19310 USA

A Word About Value

While the popularity, demand and value of vintage Hawaiian shirts has increased dramatically in the past twenty years, there are factors that have a great impact on the price a collector may pay at any given moment in time. These factors include the design and pattern, background color, number of different colors, condition, fabric, size, age, and where the shirt is purchased.

Rayon shirts made prior to the mid-1950s in Hawaii and California are the most sought after and command the highest prices. Shirts made of cotton barkcloth from Hawaii are also popular. Less valuable, but becoming popular of recent years, are rayon shits made in Japan in the 1950s. The least valuable are the cotton and polyester shirts made in Korea and China after the 1960s, unless they are from a specific designer. The economy in the areas where the demand for shirts is the highest also influences the value. At auction, should more than one bidder eagerly desire to have a shirt, it could go for several hundred dollars more than it would in a retail vintage store.

As an example, take two shirts with the identical design. One shirt is an extra large (a more difficult size to acquire), the other a small (least useable size). The extra large is a black or navy blue background (dark backgrounds are more desirable), the small a white or light gray background (less desirable). The design of the small uses three colors in the pattern while the extra large uses five colors. The small has two tiny (1/16th of an inch) holes while the large has no holes. It is conceivable that the extra large would be purchased for $600-900, while the small would not command a price higher than $200-300.

Fortunately for all collectors, there are thousands of different Hawaiian shirt designs in all price ranges from the scarcest of 1930s vintage rayons to newer collectible shirts of the past decade. Happy hunting from Gary Moss, a collector of nearly thirty years.

Note: The bold face type in the captions is the manufacturer's or retail label sewn inside the collar on each shirt. Refer to Chapter 21 for their images.

Library of Congress Cataloging-in-Publication Data:

Schiffer, Nancy.
 Hawaiian shirts : dress right for paradise / by Nancy N. Schiffer.
  p. cm.
  ISBN 0-7643-2143-9 (pbk.)
 1. Aloha shirts—Collectors and collecting. I. Title.

NK4890.S45S744 2005
687'.115—dc22
                    2004019960

Copyright © 2005 by Schiffer Publishing, Ltd.

All rights reserved. No part of this work may be reproduced or used in any form or by any means—graphic, electronic, or mechanical, including photocopying or information storage and retrieval systems—without written permission from the publisher.

The scanning, uploading and distribution of this book or any part thereof via the Internet or via any other means without the permission of the publisher is illegal and punishable by law. Please purchase only authorized editions and do not participate in or encourage the electronic piracy of copyrighted materials.

"Schiffer," "Schiffer Publishing Ltd. & Design," and the "Design of pen and ink well" are registered trademarks of Schiffer Publishing Ltd.

Designed by John P. Cheek
Cover design by Bruce Waters
Type set in Van Dijk/Humanist 521 BT

ISBN: 0-7643-2143-9
Printed in China
1 2 3 4

Endsheets. Rayon yard goods with an all-over design on a blue background showing people. The design was inspired by Eugene Savage's mural "Aloha, Universal World." *Courtesy of Dr. Gary L. Moss*
Title Page. *Left:* Hawaiian shirts design on blue background. Rayon. Marbled plastic buttons. **Campia Moda.** $50-100
Right: Hawaiian shirts design. Made in China. Silk. Blue plastic buttons. **On The Brink.** $25-50

Published by Schiffer Publishing Ltd.
4880 Lower Valley Road
Atglen, PA 19310
Phone: (610) 593-1777; Fax: (610) 593-2002
E-mail: Info@schifferbooks.com

For the largest selection of fine reference books on this and related subjects, please visit our web site at **www.schifferbooks.com**
We are always looking for people to write books on new and related subjects. If you have an idea for a book please contact us at the above address.

This book may be purchased from the publisher.
Include $3.95 for shipping.
Please try your bookstore first.
You may write for a free catalog.

In Europe, Schiffer books are distributed by
Bushwood Books
6 Marksbury Ave.
Kew Gardens
Surrey TW9 4JF England
Phone: 44 (0) 20 8392-8585; Fax: 44 (0) 20 8392-9876
E-mail: info@bushwoodbooks.co.uk
Free postage in the U.K., Europe; air mail at cost.

 Contents

Acknowledgments 4
1. Hawaii: A Glimpse of Paradise 5
2. Maps 9
3. History 17
4. Tapa 24
5. Japanese 37
6. Land of Aloha 46
7. Grass Houses 55
8. Hula 61
9. Music 70
10. Surfing 78
11. Seascapes 84
12. Fish 99
13. Birds 110
14. Trees 115
15. Landscapes 121
16. Florals 132
17. Food & Drink 167
18. Tourism 174
19. Advertising 182
20. Shirt Details 185
21. Labels 190
Recommended Reading 205
Index 206
Last Request 208

 Acknowledgments

The extensive Hawaiian shirt collection of Gary Moss served as a catalyst for this book. A brief blurb about the author on his book, *Hippie Artifacts: Mind-blowing Stuff to Collect*, includes the statement, "His collection of 150 vintage Hawaiian shirts from the 1940s is scheduled for exhibition at the American Textile Museum in Lowell, Massachusetts…" When I read that, I was stirred to contact him because we were obviously fellow enthusiasts. And so we talked and shared some common ground and the pledge to stay in touch. A later conversation convinced me that I wanted to compare some of his shirt designs with mine and explore the never-ending variety in a new book. He was enthusiastic, but compelled to be realistic about his available time to be a co-author. Dr. Gary is a busy man, as an Associate Professor at the New England College of Optometry in Boston. Soon after, however, he found he was going to be driving my way and asked if I wanted to see and photograph his shirts; if so, he would bring them along. I met him somewhere along the turnpike, where I had never been before, and we unloaded boxes, hangers, cartons, and bags full of his Hawaiian shirts into my vehicle. I now knew he was also a generous man. Thus, the book was started, the comparisons were made, and a schedule was set to complete the book. From his extensive records of recent auction sales, he has prepared the price guide. Thank you, Dr. Moss.

Another enthusiast for things Hawaiian is my old friend, a founder of the Dumpster Divers, and long-time shirt collector, Neil Benson. I told him about the new book and he offered to show me some of his new (old) shirts, including the one off his back, so we have studied them, too.

Then Mark Blackburn agreed to send me exciting shirts from his stock at Mauna Kea Gallery in Kamuela, Island of Hawaii. The varieties were growing in volume and diversity, and a story was unfolding about the evolution of images on Hawaiian shirts through the decades.

Wayne Golding, of Mambo in Australia, had contacted me in 1998 about our shared interest in "Rayon Shirts, or Loud Shirts as they're known 'wherever good rayon shirts are sold.'" I contacted him and he enthusiastically sent me Mambo shirts and the stories about the evolutions of their designs. They advanced the categories we were interested in to the near present. I can only imagine what may be coming off his design boards in the future.

A few more generous collectors, who prefer to remain anonymous, heard about the study and offered more contributions. You know who you are, and I am very grateful.

Back in the office, Bruce Waters photographed each shirt, with the assistance of Mark Bowyer, Joe Riggio, and John Fedastian. Tammy Ward efficiently helped me keep track of the pictures and prepare the captions. Jeff Snyder added the editor's touch. I couldn't have made my deadline without them.

I thank you all for your essential contributions and the fun you made out of the work involved. If I had a say, you'd be top candidates for a place in, you know, paradise. Aloha.

1. Hawaii: A Glimpse of Paradise

The name *Hawaiki*, or *Hawai'i*, derives from *hawa* (traditional home) and *iki*, or *i'i*, (small). It was the traditional home of Polynesians, according to the native inhabitants.

The Hawaiian Island chain is an archipelago stretching 1,600 miles along a fissure in the floor of the Pacific Ocean. It comprises eight major islands and 132 smaller ones. Formed by volcanoes, this island chain is the longest in the world. The Haleakala volcano on Maui is the largest inactive volcano in the world, and Kilauea, on Hawaii, is the world's largest active volcano currently. Mount Waialeale, on Kauai, is the most westerly place on earth. South Point (Ka Lae), on Hawaii, is the most southerly point in the United States.

Throughout the islands, rainforests support flowers and lush vegetation, waterfalls accentuate rivers meandering through canyons, and palm-fringed lagoons create ideal landscapes. Volcanoes and quiet mountains plunge through glorious natural gardens to serene beaches. The Pacific Ocean holds fish of many varieties to feed the people. Here there are spectacular seascapes to behold.

Into this lovely series of islands blow warm, even, tropical winds. With mountains and beaches, its temperatures can vary because of altitude, but the average beach temperature is 85 degrees Fahrenheit in summer and 78 degrees in winter.

It is not hard to understand how foreign artists were attracted to Hawaii. They popularized the place from the nineteenth century to the present and idealized the people who lived there. They proclaimed this a paradise on earth. Few have cared to disagree with them.

The men and women who have made designs, since the 1930s, for the Hawaiian textiles industry, have influenced a leisurely way of life that threatens to encompass the globe. The known, and a legion of unknown, designers have captured on cloth vignettes that reflect Hawaiian sights and traditional relaxed lifestyles. They have broadcast the luau feasts, angry volcanoes, net fishing, canoe travel, flowers, surfing, and beach life of native Hawaiians. Their textiles have been ambassadors tempting all who currently live on the planet to come and taste the old Hawaiian way of life. Hawaiian shirts are a proud part of their efforts.

All-over print with black designs inspired from Tahitian drawings by artist Paul Gauguin, in sections of yellow, purple, and pink on black ground. Designed by John Meigs (Keoni of Hawaii). **Made in Hawaii**. Selvage printed "**Kamehameha prints Made in Hawaii**." *Courtesy of Dr. Gary L. Moss.* $1,000-1,200

Island Feast menu cover. One of a series of six mural designs by Eugene Savage, used as menu covers by the Matson Line Navigation Company on their ocean liners to Hawaii in the 1940s.

Island Feast, all-over print based on Eugene Savage's mural design. **Kamehameha made and styled in Hawaii.** 1950s. *Courtesy of Dr. Gary L. Moss.* $800-1,200

Island Feast, all-over print based on Eugene Savage's mural design. Cotton. Brown marbled plastic buttons. **Ke Nui.** $400-600

Blue with white figures of active people. No pocket. Cotton. Keone of Hawaii border print. Grey plastic buttons. **Hoaloha**. $100-150

Floral, fish, and surfrider design. Rayon crepe. Long sleeves. Coconut husk buttons. **Hawaiiana, Made in Hawaii**. $175-250

Very rare shirt showing a maiden with a fruit basket on a dark blue background. Design by Frank MacIntosh for Matson Line menu covers. Rayon. Coconut husk buttons. **Kuu-Ipo.** *Courtesy of Dr. Gary L. Moss.* $1,000-1,500

"Boat Day on the Islands" with tourists and Matson cruise ship *Lurline*. Rayon. Coconut shell buttons. **Kilohana.** *Courtesy of Dr. Gary L. Moss.* $600-900

Swim shirt. Tiki border print. Two slit hip pockets. Rayon. Impressed cream plastic buttons. **Phat Farm**. $100-150

Huts, palm trees, and men fishing with nets at night on a brown background. Rayon. White shell buttons. **Saginaw**. *Courtesy of Dr. Gary L. Moss.* $175-250

Lady's Mu-Mu. Blue fish, ship, and flowers design. Cotton. **Ui Maikai**. $50-100

Neckties. Left: Rayon. Fabric marked **Blue Angel Fish Tropical Water Beauties**. Center: Rayon. **Palm Island of Miami**. Right: Rayon. Palm tree design. *Courtesy of Dr. Gary L. Moss.* $25-75 each

2. Maps

The 132 smaller islands of the Hawaiian chain, northwest of Kauai, are not generally shown on maps of Hawaii today. From west to east, the eight major islands of the Hawaiian chain are Niihau, Kauai, Oahu, Molokai, Lanai, Kahoolawe, Maui, and Hawaii. Kauai is the oldest of the islands, about 5.6 million years, and Hawaii is the youngest; it is still forming. Together, these eight comprise 4,038 square miles of land. New lands formed by lava flows belong to the state, not abutting property owners, according to a ruling by the Hawaii Supreme Court in 1977.

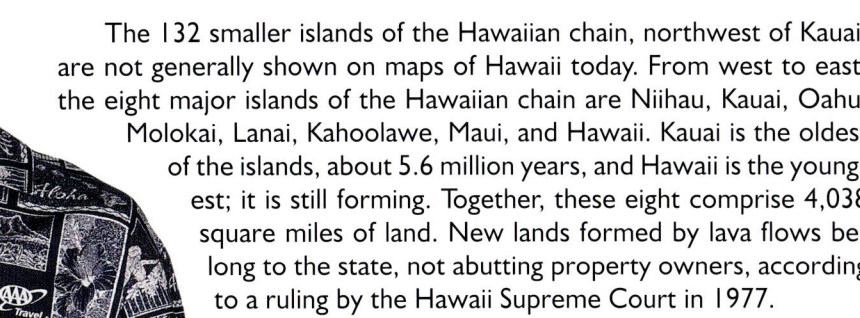

Pleasant Hawaiian Holidays. AAA Travel design. Cotton. Blue plastic buttons. **Hilo Hattie.** $25-50

White with black "Chart of the Hawaiian Isles." Polyester and cotton. White plastic buttons. **Made in Hawaii.** $25-50

Aqua floral on white border print. Hawaiian travel design. Cotton bark cloth. White plastic buttons. **Tropicana**. $50-100

Blue "Chart of the Hawaiian Isles." Slit pocket. Polyester and cotton. White plastic buttons. **Orchid Fashions**. $25-50

The 50th State. Cotton. White plastic inscribed Billabong buttons. **Billabong**. $25-50

Hawaiian map. Brown. Rayon. **Khaki Safau**. $50-100

Blue map of Hawaii. Polyester and cotton. White plastic buttons. **Howie**. $25-50

Turquoise map of Hawaii. Cotton. Molded gold plastic buttons. **Ui-Maikai**. $25-50

Map of Hawaiian Islands with hibiscus, fish, pineapple. Cotton. Stamped silver plastic buttons with squares design. **Ui-Maikai**. $25-50

Blue map of Hawaii. Rayon. Blue plastic buttons. **Marcdaniels**. $50-100

Blue map design with gold edges. Made in Waikiki. Cotton. Silver molded plastic buttons. **Tina Fashions**. $25-50

Hawaiian scenes and map. Cotton. Molded silver plastic impressed buttons. Aloha Hawaii. **Hawaiian Holiday Sports Wear**. $50-100

Map of Hawaii with trees and flowers. Rayon. Brown plastic buttons. **Route 66**. $25-50

Blue islands design. Cotton. White plastic buttons. **Tamaré**. $25-50

Chart of Hawaiian Islands. Rayon. **Made in Hawaii**. $25-50

Whale and Hawaiian islands design. Polyester. Cloth covered buttons. **Pacific Isle Creations**. $25-50

Hawaiian Islands and palm trees design on blue background. Cotton. Wooden buttons. **Krush Hawaii.** *$25-50*

Whales and Hawaiian Islands design. Polyester. White plastic buttons. **Fashioned by Hukilao Fashions**. $25-50

All-over Hawaii and Oahu islands design with girl and King Kamehameha statue on black ground. **Kanoi Koi Golden Gate Sportswear**. *Courtesy of Dr. Gary L. Moss.* $300-500

Street map of Waikiki Beach at Honolulu including hotels and Outrigger Canoe Club location on yellow background. Coconut shell buttons. **Made and Styled in Honolulu, Hawaii**. *Courtesy of Dr. Gary L. Moss*. $400-600

Map and nautical compass design. Polyester. **Pacific Isle Creations**. $25-50

Child's shirt with blue background and chart of the Hawaiian Islands. No pocket. White plastic buttons. **Cut off**. $25-50

Map of the Hawaiian Islands. Slit pocket. Cotton. White plastic buttons. **Shoreline Hawaii**. $25-50

Child's shirt with Hawaiian map design. Cotton. White plastic buttons. **Nui Nalu**. $25-50

Aqua background with blue islands design and gold edges. Cotton. Pressed gold metal buttons. $50-100

Tropical scenes and map of island group "SavuSavu..." on shaded yellow background. Rayon. Brown marbled plastic buttons. **Pazzo**. $25-50

3. History

Marquesan settlers arrived on the Hawaiian Islands about 750 AD and were followed by Tahitian settlers up to 500 years later. Here they conducted life among the islands without a written language. Their oral traditions served as history as well as wisdom for the population.

In the winter of 1778, British Captain James Cook (?-1779) sailed to the Waimea shore on Kauai with the *HMS Resolution* and the *HMS Discovery*. He named the Hawai'ian islands after the Earl of Sandwich, First Lord of Admiralty (who also had originated the food item sandwich). They were called the Sandwich Islands until about 1850, when the name became obsolete.

The famous King Kamehameha I (-1819) was a young man of royalty who accompanied his uncle, Kalaniopuu, king of the island of Hawaii, aboard Captain Cook's ships in 1778 and 1779. There he learned the power of gunfire. When his uncle died in 1782, Kamehameha fought with other groups on the big island until 1790. With the aid of two former British sailors, he assembled an arsenal of guns and ammunition and conquered Maui and Molokai. Other battles raged until he retook Maui and Molokai in 1794 and Oahu in 1795, thus establishing his kingdom. In 1812, Kamehameha I retired to a peaceful life until his death in 1819.

The famous statue of Kamehameha was ordered by King David Kalakaua (1836-1891) for Honolulu and was cast in Florence, Italy. Lost at sea near the Falkland Islands, it was later recovered and placed at Kapaau, Kohala, Hawaii, the legendary birthplace of Kamehameha. Another casting, made after the original was lost, is in Honolulu at the Iolani Palace, and a copy is at the Capitol in Washington, D.C., made in 1969 to represent the state of Hawaii.

By 1820, travelers and immigrants from Britain, Scotland, France, Italy, Spain, Portugal, China, and America were living in Hawaii. Sugar cane was planted as a cash crop by some of the immigrants. The native population was dying out because of Western diseases. Also by 1820, missionaries standardized a 12-letter alphabet for the Hawaiian language, comprised of the five vowels (a, e, i, o, u) and seven consonants (h, k, l, m, n, p, w). Thereby, the oral language was committed to a strict written form.

Planters imported 300 Chinese laborers for the sugar plantations in 1852 and 1853. Over the years, thousands more followed. The first Portuguese workers arrived in 1883 and about 1,300 German workers came during that time. From 1868 to 1924, around 200,000 Japanese laborers came to Hawaii to work the developing industries. Hawaiians were outnumbered in the population by 1886. In the early twentieth century, 5,000 Puerto Ricans and 7,500 Koreans arrived in Hawaii to work and live, followed by Filipinos and Okinawans. Hawaii had become the melting pot of the Pacific.

Plantation workers in Hawaii typically wore a standard work shirt called a *palaka* until the second decade of the twentieth century. They were made of blue and white denim plaid cloth with a buttoned front, turned collar, and long sleeves. These were commercially made and withstood years of hearty use in the open agricultural fields.

In 1894, after years of political turmoil, Hawaii became a Republic, and in 1898 it became an official Territory of the United States. Hawaii was an important location in the vast Pacific Ocean for U. S. military activities in the early twentieth century that culminated in the naval base at Pearl Harbor.

Hawaii became the 50th state to join the United States in 1959. Many American men and women, who toured through Hawaii as service personnel, returned years later on pleasure vacations. They became part of the tourist trade that superseded agriculture as Hawaii's top industry by the 1960s. Their enthusiasm for Hawaiian shirts, bought in Hawaii and worn in the continental 48 states, helped to popularize the style.

Before long, textile companies on the mainland and across the world were making Hawaiian-style shirts for leisure wear. Their designs often derived from Hawaiian traditions and images of Hawaiian culture, both real and imagined.

The King Kamehameha statue in Honolulu.

All-over "Kamehameha Hawaii" design on yellow background. Coconut shell buttons. **Surfriders.** *Courtesy of Dr. Gary L. Moss.* $400-600

Picture print on blue ground showing pineapple planter, Honolulu skyline, King Kamehameha statue, and palm tree climber. Coconut husk buttons in horizontal holes. **An original by Hale Hawaii Made in Hawaii.** *Courtesy Mauna Kea Gallery, Kamuela, Hawaii.* $600-900

All-over labeled scenes on blue ground: "Alohanui," "Paradise Isles," "Mauka," Ala Wai," "Waikiki." Dark coconut buttons in vertical holes. **Japanese Bazaar Honolulu Made in Hawaii**. *Courtesy Mauna Kea Gallery, Kamuela, Hawaii.* $800-1,200

Hawaiian insignia and pineapple design. Bark cloth. Slit pocket. White plastic buttons. **Tropicana Hawaii**. $100-150

All-over print inspired by the design *Aloha, A Universal Word,* by Eugene Savage, of King Kamehameha wearing a ceremonial helmet and with women attendants and banana leaves on a red ground. **Made and Styled in Honolulu Hawaii**. *Courtesy of Dr. Gary L. Moss.* $500-700

Hawaiian insignia horizontal design. Bark cloth. Cotton. White plastic buttons. **Penny's Hawaii**. $100-150

All-over stylized floral, fan, and Hawaiian crest design on black ground. **Holiday Sportswear**. *Courtesy of Dr. Gary L. Moss.* $600-900

"Royal Kahili" insignia on black background. Rayon. Long sleeves and black plastic buttons. **Manhattan Sportswear.** *Courtesy of Dr. Gary L. Moss.* $300-500

King Kamehalneha design on blue background. No pocket. Rayon. Brown plastic buttons. **Creative Edge**. $50-100

"Hawaii Kahilis" insignia on lime green background. Rayon. Black plastic buttons. **Kuonakakai.** *Courtesy of Dr. Gary L. Moss.* $300-500

All-over insignia including feather kahilis and capes on a yellow tapa design. Yellow plastic buttons. *Courtesy of Dr. Gary L. Moss.* $100-150

Yellow Polynesian design. Slit pocket. Polyester. White plastic buttons. **Tropicana**. $25-50

Crepe all-over print, Royal group on double canoe barge and cremonial equipment, on simulated tie-dyed blue ground. Coconut husk buttons in horizontal holes. **Sewn expressly for Peggy & Johnny's Made in Hawaii.** *Courtesy Mauna Kea Gallery, Kamuela, Hawaii.* $800-1,200

Orange kahili, cape, and drum design on cracked white background. Slit pocket. Polyester. White plastic buttons. **Malihini Hawaii Liberty House of Hawaii.** $25-50

All-over Hawaiian activity designs labeled on a green ground. "Hukilau" net fishermen, "Ho'pwali Poi" pounding poi, "Na wa'a ona alii" canoe race, "'Ahu'ula" chief's cape, "Pa'I kappa" making tapa cloth. Coconut shell buttons in horizontal holes. **Watumull's Honolulu, Hawaii.** *Courtesy Mauna Kea Gallery, Kamuela, Hawaii.* $800-1,200

All-over yellow and brown Hawaiian activity designs labeled on a black ground. "Hukilau" net fishermen, "Ho'pwali Poi" pounding poi, "Na wa'a ona alii" canoe race, "'Ahu'ula" chief's cape, "Pa'I kappa" making tapa cloth. Coconut shell buttons in horizontal holes. **Watumull's Honolulu, Hawaii.** *Courtesy of Dr. Gary L. Moss.* $600-900

All-over Maheoli design on burgundy background lettered, "Hawaiian Pua" and "Maheoli." Coconut hull buttons. **Made in Hawaii for Ross Sutherland Honolulu.** *Courtesy of Dr. Gary L. Moss.* $600-900

Cotton handkerchief souvenir, 1950s.

Iolani Palace, the capitol building in Honolulu.

Blue cotton denim printed with white "Matsonia" and Iolani Palace drawing design. White plastic buttons. $25-50

 # 4. Tapa

Clothing in Hawaii was considered a rather optional concern until the western missionaries arrived in 1819. Traditionally, the natives made a bark cloth (*kappa*) from the paper of the mulberry tree by pounding the wood fibers and bleaching them in the sun. They produced strips two inches wide and about four feet long, which they joined into a material, called *tapa*, to make a garment. Men wore a loincloth (*malo*) and women wore a skirt (*pau*). Tapa capes were worn over the shoulders to keep warm.

The tapa cloth was frequently colored with juice from the kukui nut tree to produce a uniform yellow background, and then was stamped with red or yellow ochre and charcoal in geometric designs. These tapa designs formed the basis for textile designs in Hawaii and have been augmented with many additional patterns over the years. Hawaiian shirts with tapa designs have been popular since the 1930s.

Early, traditional tapa designs

Red squares of tapa design on a geometric background. Rayon. White plastic buttons. **Malibo Crepe.** *Courtesy of Dr. Gary L. Moss.* $175-250

Brown and yellow tapa design with four leaves in a square. Brown plastic buttons. *Courtesy of Dr. Gary L. Moss.* $100-150

Swim trunks. Yellow. Cotton. Coconut shell buttons. **Duke Kahanahmoku by Catalina**. $25-50

Matching swim trunks. *Courtesy of Dr. Gary L. Moss.* $50-100

Yellow tapa design. Rayon. Brown plastic buttons. **Duke Kahanamoku by Catalina California, USA**. $50-100

Squares of butterfly and tulip design on yellow background. Yellow plastic buttons. **Tropicana**. *Courtesy of Dr. Gary L. Moss.* $250-400

Yellow geometric design on brown background. Cotton bark cloth with white plastic buttons. Late 1950s. *Courtesy of Dr. Gary L. Moss.* $100-150

Horizonral brown and yellow floral. Slit pocket. Cotton. Bark cloth. **Kole Kole Hawaii**. $100-150

Brown tapa design. Faded rayon. White plastic buttons. **Made in Hawaii for Andrade Honolulu**. $100-150

Orange tappa design. Slit pocket. Cotton. Brown plastic buttons. **Barefoot in Paradise**. $50-100

Multi-colored geometric design. Cotton bark cloth. **Island Creations**. $25-50

Child's shirt. Geometric tapa variation in green and orange. Cotton bark cloth. Molded gold plastic buttons. **Made in Hawaii**. $50-100

Swim trunks. Green geometric design. Cotton. **Kuna Kai by Jantzen**. $25-50

Brown tapa design. Cotton bark cloth. White plastic buttons. **Pomare Tahiti**. $50-100

Bark cloth. Cotton. Large white plastic buttons. **The King Size Co.** $25-50

Green tapa design. Cotton bark cloth. White plastic buttons. **Sears Sportswear**. $50-100

Yellow geometric and cat design. Cotton. Beige plastic buttons. **Coopers Sport Shirt**. $25-50

Blue floral/tapa design. Rayon. **Sears Sportswear for Pool, Beach and Patio**. $25-50

Bark cloth. Rayon. White plastic buttons. **Towncraft Designer Collection JC Penney**. $25-50

Geometric design. Cotton. Blue plastic buttons. **Kona Kai by Jantzen**. $25-50

Blue tapa design. Vertical. Cotton bark cloth. Selvage JAHACA Print Design No. K2347. **Made in Hawaii**. $50-100

Blue tapa and floral design. Cotton. Coconut husk buttons. **Kamehameha**. $25-50

Blue tapa print. Cotton. Black plastic buttons. **Kona Kai by Jantzen**. $25-50

Swim trunks. Blue and white tapa, Hawaiian spear fisherman, and pineapple design. Cotton. **The Kahala Made in Honolulu**. $25-50

Cotton with vertical geometric print in red on dark pink ground. Coconut shell buttons in vertical holes. **Styled and Made in Hawaii Kahana Manufacturing Co. Honolulu.** *Courtesy of Dr. Gary L. Moss.* $100-150

Brown geometric print on dark blue background. Cotton with white terry cloth lining. White plastic buttons. **Sea Island Swimwear**. $25-50

Green vertical tapa design. Cotton. Molded gold plastic buttons. **Royal Hawaiian**. $50-100

Vertical green tapa design. Cotton. Molded gold plastic buttons. **Ui-Maikai**. $25-50

Vertical rows of tapa design. Bark cloth. Cotton. Coconut shell buttons. **Tapa Design Hawaii**. $25-50

Dark vertical tapa and sailboat design. Small black plastic buttons. **Hawaii Blues**. $25-50

Horizontal geometric design. Cotton and rayon. Molded gold plastic buttons. **Sears Hawaiian Fashions**. $25-50

Abstract plaid design on yellow background. Coconut husk buttons. **Deer Creek.** *Courtesy of Dr. Gary L. Moss.* $100-150

Patches with people on white background with squiggle pattern. Rayon. White plastic buttons. *Courtesy of Dr. Gary L. Moss.* $250-400

Horizontal tapa, peace symbol, and geometric designs on yellow patterned ground. **Bai Nani Hawaii.** 1960s. *Courtesy of Dr. Gary L. Moss.* $100-150

Palm trees and maze pattern on yellow background. Rayon. White plastic buttons. **Terrace Club.** *Courtesy of Dr. Gary L. Moss.* $100-150

Border print. Cotton. Shell buttons. **Club.** $50-100

All-over red decorated ovals design on dark green background. Rayon with long sleeves. White plastic buttons. **Champion Kahanamoku.** *Courtesy of Dr. Gary L. Moss.* $250-400

Swim Shirt. Blue and geometric design. Cotton bark cloth. Silver molded metal buttons. Zipper front. **Mukai Fashions.** $50-100

Medallions of colorful geometric design on green background. Rayon. Black plastic buttons. **Tropicool Sportswear.** *Courtesy of Dr. Gary L. Moss.* $250-400

All-over rectangular panels with gold decoration on light blue ground. **Polynesian Casuals for Ross Sutherland Hawaii**. 1950s. *Courtesy of Dr. Gary L. Moss.* $100-150

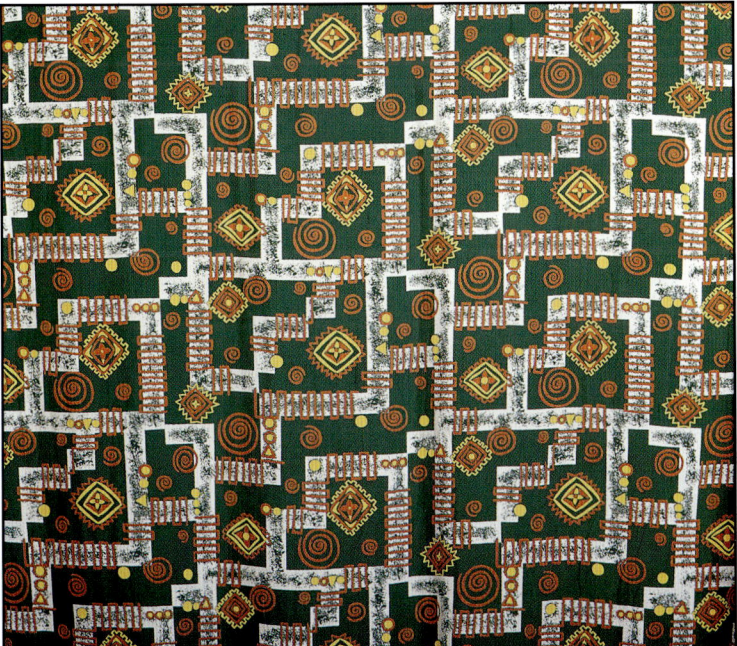

Rayon yard goods printed with colorful geometric designs on green ground.

Vertical border print of stripes and star fruit on a white background. Rayon. White plastic buttons. **Champion Kahanamoku Made by Cisco**. *Courtesy of Dr. Gary L. Moss.* $250-400

Tapa design by Martin Plaza, 1996. **Mambo**. $75-150

Border print with colored squares and crossed patches on dark blue background. Black plastic buttons. **Catalina A California Creator**. *Courtesy of Dr. Gary L. Moss.* $175-250

Two rectangular landscapes in patterned red frames on yellow ground. **McGregor**. Silk, 1950s. *Courtesy of Dr. Gary L. Moss.* $175-250

5. Japanese

Japanese and Chinese tailors in Hawaii in the 1930s imported printed silk and cotton cloth from Japan to make up into kimono for their Asian clients. When some of the more enterprising of their group began making colorful shirts from this cloth for the beach boys of Hawaii, the shirts started to sell well. Eventually, tourists took up the flare and before long, by 1936, a small industry was underway in Hawaii. Koichiro Miyamoto, known as Musa Shiya the Shirtmaker, and Ellery Chun were among the earliest group, and they boldly advertised their new style in Honolulu newspapers in 1935 and 1936.

Some of the most dramatic Hawaiian shirts have portrayed designs typical of Japanese culture. Beautifully printed birds, Japanese mountains, landscapes, symbols, pagodas, and kimono-clad people appear on Hawaiian shirts that may have been designed or manufactured in Japan or be intended for Japanese customers.

Hawaiian shirts made on the mainland in the early 1950s often were printed in the "chop suey" style, having many small Hawaiian designs scattered on a plain background.

All-over crane, fan, and sail of a junk design on purple ground. No label. Japanese silk. Vertical button holes. *Courtesy of Dr. Gary L. Moss.* $175-250

Horizontal "Aloha Week Hawaii" parade design with dark blue background. Coconut shell buttons. **Tropicana**. *Courtesy of Dr. Gary L. Moss.* $400-600

Rayon with one scene of a Japanese footbridge over a stream on gray ground. Coconut husk buttons in horizontal holes. **Musashiya Ltd. Honolulu.** *Courtesy of Dr. Gary L. Moss.* $600-900

Long sleeve silk with all-over Japanese style calligraphy and writing tools, bonsai tree, and scrolls designs on light brown ground. Beige plastic buttons painted with floral decoration in vertical holes. **Machin Shirtmaker Los Angeles.** *Courtesy of Dr. Gary L. Moss.* $100-150

No pocket, open weave cloth, Ying/Yang design. Black plastic buttons. **Taboo**. $50-100

No pocket. Polyester. Blue plastic buttons. **Trust**. $25-50

Japanese dancer. Black buttons. **Phat Farm**. $25-50

Polyester. NLMT tag on side of pocket. Blue plastic inscribed "No Limit" buttons. **N LMT Urban equipment**. $25-50

Chinese landscape on black. No pocket. Rayon. White plastic buttons. **Lucky Beach**. $25-50

Blue dragon design. No pocket. Rayon. Marbled plastic buttons. **Presence Clothing**. $25-50

Emblem on pocket with pen compartment. Rayon. Black plastic inscribed Phat Farm buttons. **Phat Farm est. 1992**. $25-50

Rayon. White plastic buttons. Lucky Beach Hula wear. **Paradise Found**. $50-100

Black koi fish and Japanese lettering. Rayon. Brown plastic buttons. **Marro Bay**. $50-100

Japanese pagoda and cranes. Rayon and cotton. Dark brown wood buttons. **D.F. Clothing Co. Dragonfly**. $25-50

Woman's blouse. Japanese pagodas. No pocket. Rayon. Shell buttons. **CLIO**. $50-100

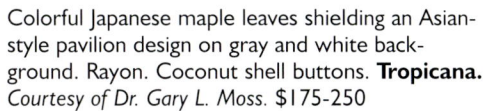

Colorful Japanese maple leaves shielding an Asian-style pavilion design on gray and white background. Rayon. Coconut shell buttons. **Tropicana**. *Courtesy of Dr. Gary L. Moss.* $175-250

Traditional kimono cloth design of Japanese artifacts. Silk, with long sleeves. **Andrade.** *Courtesy of Dr. Gary L. Moss.* $100-150

Dragon design. Made in Korea. Rayon. Small black plastic buttons. **Monticerutti.** $50-100

Vertical serpent fighting a tiger design on dark brown background. Rayon. Yellow plastic buttons. **Malihini.** *Courtesy of Dr. Gary L. Moss.* $1,800-2,400

Japanese dragon and "American colors" design in orange. Cotton. Brown/purple? inscribed plastic buttons. **American Colors.** $25-50

Tiger and landscape design on blue crackled background. Rayon. White shell buttons. **Made in Japan.** *Courtesy of Dr. Gary L. Moss.* $400-600

Tiger design. Polyester. Made in Korea. Grey plastic incised buttons. **Phat Farm New York**. $25-50

"Tropicana" design by Jim Mitchell, 2001. Rayon. Coconut shell buttons. **Mambo**. $75-150

"Manonoke" design by Rockin' Jelly Bean, 2001. Rayon. Japanese dramatic figures. Coconut shell buttons. **Mambo**. $75-150

Dragon design. Rayon. Coconut shell buttons. **Mambo**. $75-150

Border print Chinese landscape with rickshaw design on white background. Rayon. White plastic buttons. *Courtesy of Dr. Gary L. Moss.* $100-150

Vertical strips of different cloth designs. Rayon. White plastic buttons. **Lucky Beach**. $50-100

6. Land of Aloha

Images of traditional Hawaiian life abound among the shirts and some include Hawaiian words as part of the design. These are among the most frequently used Hawaiian words:

Hawaiian	English
ali'i	chief, royalty
aloha	hello, goodbye, love
hale	house
hana	work
haole	white person
holoku	formal gown with a train
holomu	formal gown without a train
hui	club
hukilau	group net fishing
hula	Hawaiian dance
kai	ocean
kahuna	priest, expert
kama'aina	native person
kane	man
kappa	bark cloth
kapu	taboo
kapuna	ancestors, elders
keiki	child
lanai	porch, balcony
lei	garland
lua	bathroom
lu'au	Hawaiian feast
mahalo	thank you
malihini	foreigner
mana	supernatural power
mauna	mountain
mele	song
muumuu	informal dress
oli	chant
pali	cliff
paniolo	cowboy
pu'u	hill
tutu	grandmother
wahine	woman
wai	fresh water

All-over "Hawaii Land of Aloha" design. Crepe, made in four colors. **Hale Hawaii.** *Courtesy of Dr. Gary L. Moss.* $400-600

Woman's halter style dress with wrap-around skirt in "Hawaii Land of Aloha" design with hula girls and the Hawaiian crest. **Hale Hawaii.** *Courtesy of Dr. Gary L. Moss.* $250-400

All-over "Hawaii Land of Aloha" design on light blue background. Coconut shell buttons. **Hale Hawaii.** *Courtesy of Dr. Gary L. Moss.* $500-700

Blue "Hawaii Land of Aloha" banner. Cotton. Blue plastic buttons. **Le Tigré**. $25-50

Red "Hawaii Land of Aloha" design. White plastic buttons. Made in Thailand. **Koko Knot by In Gear Fashions.** $25-50

Child's shirt in "Land of Aloha" print design including girls giving leis to a businessman with a suitcase, the Aloha tower, and palm trees. Rayon. **Malihini Made in Hawaii**. *Courtesy of Dr. Gary L. Moss.* $100-150

Aloha sunset. Rayon and cotton. Marbled plastic buttons. **Impaq Hawaii**. $25-50

Blue "Hawaii Land of Aloha" banner. Rayon. Marbled plastic buttons. **B J Bay Sports**. $25-50

Green "Aloha Hawaii." Cotton. Molded gold metal buttons. **Made in Hawaii**. $25-50

Black with Hawaiian images. Rayon. Black plastic buttons. **Margenata**. $25-50

"Aloha Hawaii" island and water design. Made in Taiwan. Polyester and cotton. White plastic buttons. **Designed in Hawaii. Calabash Products**. $25-50

Green floral. Polyester. Coconut shell. **Made in Hawaii**. $25-50

Orange landscape. Slit pocket. Cotton. Fabric covered buttons. **Pacific Isle Creations**. $25-50

Green, words Hawaii Aloha. Cotton. White plastic buttons. **Address Unknown**.

Hawaiian place names and images, including hula dancers, on yellow ground. Coconut husk buttons. **Kamehameha.** *Courtesy of Dr. Gary L. Moss.* $500-700

Hawaiian words design. Rayon cotton and linens. Coconut shell buttons. **John Severson Collection by Kahula**. $50-100

Muumuu of "Aloha Hawaii" design. Rayon. **Island Fashions.** *Courtesy of Dr. Gary L. Moss.* $25-50

Robe of kimono style with white Hawaiian scenes and words on a green background. Rayon. *Courtesy of Dr. Gary L. Moss.* $100-150

All-over "Lei Queen" and "Pao Riders" ceremonial design on gray background. Black plastic buttons. **Watumulls**. *Courtesy of Dr. Gary L. Moss.* $500-700

"Aloha Kakou" fish and bananas design on speckled brown background. Cotton. **The Liberty House Waikiki.** *Courtesy of Dr. Gary L. Moss.* $250-400

All-over "Aloha Hawaii" design on medium green background. Cream plastic buttons. **Saginaw**. *Courtesy of Dr. Gary L. Moss.* $400-600

Aloha Hawaii souvenir pillow cover from 1943. *Courtesy of Dr. Gary L. Moss*

All-over design of starfish, flowers, square, and sailboats, "Aloha Hawaii." White plastic buttons. **Made in California**. *Courtesy of Dr. Gary L. Moss.* $400-600

Aloha Hawaii design. Cotton. Bark cloth. Molded silver plastic buttons. **Made in Hawaii**. $50-100

Hawaii and Aloha posters. Rayon. **First Down Southern Rim**. $25-50

Hawaiian Christmas design. Cotton and polyester. Marbled brown plastic buttons. **Code Sheet Honolulu**. $25-50

7. Grass Houses

The fantasy of living in a little grass house next to a blue lagoon in paradise lives on in Hawaiian shirt designs.

A little grass shack in Hawaii.

Horizontal print of thatched huts by the ocean, palm tree, ferns, and bathers on dark green ground. White shell buttons in horizontal holes. **Champion Kahanamoku an Hawaiian original.** *Courtesy Mauna Kea Gallery, Kamuela, Hawaii.* $800-1,200

Tiki heads. Cotton. Marbled plastic buttons. **Peppermint Bay New York**. $25-50

Hawaiian scenes. Rayon. Brown plastic buttons. **Pineapple Connection**. $25-50

Pink Hawaiian landscape. Cotton. Marbled plastic. **JJ Cochran**. $25-50

Grass huts on yellow. Made in Korea. Silk. Coconut shell buttons. **American Archives**. Classic shirts authentic Twentieth Century print, hand screened and printed on 100 percent silk. $100-150

Yellow. Palm trees. Coconut shell and husk buttons. **K.A.D. Clothing Co.** $25-50

All-over palm tree design with drawings of grass huts and bowls of fruit on green ground. **Pennleigh Hand washable.** 1940s. *Courtesy of Dr. Gary L. Moss.* $175-250

Blue vertical Hawaiian design. Cotton. Molded silver plastic buttons and matching hem buttons. $25-50

Vertical floral and palm tree rows. Bark cloth. Cotton. Coconut husk buttons. **odo.** $25-50

Landscape with grass houses. Cotton. Brown plastic buttons. **Peppermint Bay**. $25-50

All-over landscape design with children on a beach and bonfire, grass hut, and hula dancers on red background. **Royal Hawaiian Made and styled in Hawaii**.
Courtesy of Dr. Gary L. Moss. $150-225

Grass huts, palm trees, and hula dancers "Aloha" design on light blue background. Rayon. Coconut shell buttons. **Royal Hawaiian.**
Courtesy of Dr. Gary L. Moss. $150-225

Border print with landscape and distant water activities on dark blue background. Rayon. White plastic buttons. **Champion Kahanamoku.**
Courtesy of Dr. Gary L. Moss. $500-700

Temple with thatched roof and red leaves design on patchy dark blue background. Rayon. White plastic buttons. **Hookano.** *Courtesy of Dr. Gary L. Moss.* $175-250

Cotton. Yellow plastic buttons. **GAP**. $25-50

Slot pocket. Polyester. White plastic buttons. **Kai Nani Hawaii**. $25-50

Buildings and palm trees on blue water background. Rayon. White plastic buttons. **Made in Japan**. *Courtesy of Dr. Gary L. Moss.* $50-100

Hat. Brown Hawaiian print. Cotton. **Campus**.

Green, long sleeves, no pocket. Rayon. White plastic buttons. **Mitford**. $25-50

Placket front, grass shack and outriggers design. Cotton. Kahala tag at side of pocket. Brown plastic buttons. **Kahala**. $50-100

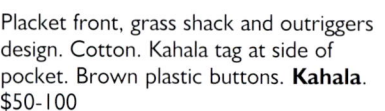

8. Hula

Hula dancers are specially trained to perform traditional stories to music through hand and body movements. They generally perform wearing a skirt of ti leaves or tapa skirts (pa'u) and leis.

Hula dancers with a Hawaiian band and poi pounder.

All-over "Hula" dancer design on blue ground. Long sleeves. **Hale Hawaii**. *Courtesy of Dr. Gary L. Moss.* $600-900

Vertical border print of flowers and woman's head on a light chartreuse background. Coconut shell buttons. **Leilani Honolulu**. *Courtesy of Dr. Gary L. Moss.* $800-1,200

Blue with hula girls. Rayon. Coconut shell buttons. **Hilo Hattie**. $50-100

Hula dancer and hibiscus design. Rayon. White plastic buttons. **Lucky Beach**. $100-150

A fine *holoku* gown worn by a hula dancer.

Hula dancer in a long gown design on a black background. No pocket. Rayon. Marbled plastic. **Thums Up for Him**. $50-100

Floral and hula dancer. Rayon. Coconut shell buttons. **Palm Bay**. aaaaa425-50

Boy child's all-over Hawaiian scenes on printed woven squares and dark blue ground. Yellow plastic buttons in horizontal holes. **Kahili Sportswear Made in Hawaii.** *Courtesy Mauna Kea Gallery, Kamuela, Hawaii.* $300-500

The uli uli dance.

Necktie. Blue hula dancers design. Silk. $50-100

All-over leis, ukuleles, palm trees, and hula dancers design on blue ground. No label. 3-button placket with loop button fasteners. *Courtesy of Dr. Gary L. Moss.* $300-500

Greeting card in the shape of a Hawaiian shirt with a wire hanger. Paper and wire. 2002. **Hallmark.**

Necktie. Island scenes with Hawaiian labels on brown/red background. Silk. Selvage of fabric marked: "Ola Ainapuluwai" Reyn Sponner, Inc., ©1994. **ADOLFO**. $25-50

Blue luau design. Rayon. Coconut shell buttons. **Made in USA**. $50-100

Hilo Hattie performing a dance.

Black background hula dancer. Marbled plastic buttons. **Thums Up for Him**. $50-100

Yellow with palm trees. Made in Japan. Rayon. White plastic buttons. **S.R. CLIFFORD Holiday Wear**. $50-100

Blue squares with Hawaiian designs. Polyester and cotton. Placket front. **Pride of Hawaii**. $50-100

Necktie. Tropical posters design. Silk. **Chaps Ralph Lauren**. $25-50

Hula dancers.

Border print, hula girls and banana plants. Cotton. **Hilo Hattie**. $100-150

Woman's pants. Aqua tropical design. Cotton and rayon. **OP Montabert**. $25-50

Hula Baby design by Steve Bliss, 1996. Rayon. Coconut shell buttons. **Mambo**.

"Body Parts, Custom Accessories" design. Rayon. Coconut shell buttons. **Mambo**. $75-150

9. Music

Ancient Hawaiians used various sound-producing instruments, some for their musical qualities and others for beating time to the movements of hula dances. They used bamboo flutes, wooden drums with sharkskin covers, and shell trumpets. Bamboo and gourds were used in connection with different hula dances. Later, ukuleles and slak-key guitars were introduced by European immigrants, and today they are intrinsically connected with Hawaiian folk music. Many of the most popular songs over the years were written by Hawaiian kings and queens to celebrate their people.

All-over print of Japanese flute and drum on dark green ground. No label. *Courtesy of Dr. Gary L. Moss.* $300-500

Dark blue drums on crackled background. Slit pocket. Cotton. White plastic buttons. **Tropicana Made in Honolulu**. $100-150

Swim trunks. Blue with drums design. Cotton. **Napili Made in Hawaii**. $25-50

Tiki design. Bark cloth. Cotton. Molded gold plastic buttons. **Fashioned By Hakihu Fashion Honolulu**. $100-150

Sombreros, drums, and musical instrument on white background. Seersucker with two chest pockets with flaps. Brown plastic buttons. **B.V.D. Brand.** *Courtesy of Dr. Gary L. Moss.* **$175-250**

Musical notes and words to a hula song. "Lovely hula hands..." Metal Griffin buttons. **Bun Fashions of Hawaii**. $50-100

Hula girls. Rayon. White marble plastic buttons. **Campia**. $25-50

"Hawaii" with flowers, drums, and ukulele design on dark blue background. Rayon with long sleeves and white plastic buttons. **Kulani Beach Tropical Sportswear**. $300-500

Guitars, violins, ukuleles, drums, and gourds design. Polyester. Orange plastic buttons. **Box Office Island**. $25-50

Back panel of ukulele player on white ground, with canoe paddle, ukulele, and leis on lower front right panel. Old clear plastic buttons (yellowed) in horizontal holes. **Aloha Kanaka Original by Artvogue**. *Courtesy Mauna Kea Gallery, Kamuela, Hawaii.* $800-1,200

White flowers and ukuleles on brown background. Rayon. Coconut shell buttons. **Westwood Casuals.** *Courtesy of Dr. Gary L. Moss.* $600-900

Ukulele and floral design on black background. White plastic buttons. No label. *Courtesy of Dr. Gary L. Moss.* $600-900

Ukulele and flowers design. Rayon. Coconut shell buttons. **Bruno**. $50-100

Floral with drums and tiki heads. Rayon. Black plastic buttons. **Montage Tropics**. $50-100

Woman's blouse. "I had to lova and leva on the lava" all-over design on red ground. **Helen's Wailuka Maui.** *Courtesy of Dr. Gary L. Moss.* $300-500

Jazz musicians design. Cotton. Small white shell buttons. **Bullock & Jones San Francisco.** $25-50

Flower and ukulele design. Rayon. Blue plastic buttons. **Mambo**. $75-150

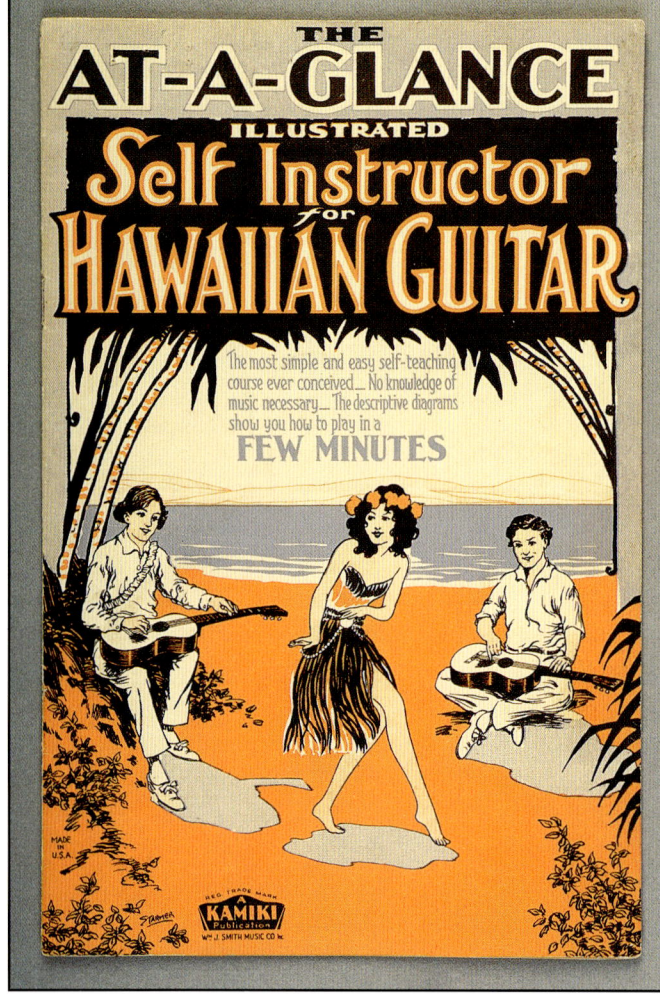

Cover of a guitar instructional booklet.

"Bongo Floral" design by Jim Mitchell, 1997. Rayon. Coconut shell buttons. **Mambo**. $75-150

All-over drum and shield design on light blue ground. **Andrade Sport Shops Honolulu**. Silk. *Courtesy of Dr. Gary L. Moss.* $150-200

Gray Mid-Pacific Carnival. Rayon. Brown plastic buttons. **Pazzo**. $25-50

10. Surfing

In the old days, wave sliding (*he'e nalu*), now known as surf riding or just surfing, was a sport reserved for Hawaiian royalty on their exclusive beaches. Hawaiian Olympic swimmer "Duke" Paoa Kahanamoku introduced the Hawaiian sport of surf riding to California and the West in the early 1900s. By the 1950s, a surfing culture was part of the California lifestyle. Today, the sport is enjoyed the world over by men and women alike.

All-over surfboarders and the sea design. 1930s. Coconut shell buttons. **Paradise Sportswear.** *Courtesy of Dr. Gary L. Moss.* $1,000-1,500

Wooden plaque enameled with a surfing scene at Waikiki Beach in Honolulu. *Courtesy of Dr. Gary L. Moss*

Surfing and net fisherman design. No pocket. Cotton. Reverse side of cloth used. Brown plastic buttons. **American Blue Authentics**. $25-50

Vertical rows of floral and surfer designs. Rayon. Coconut husk buttons. **Marc Edwards**. $25-50

Post cards. Rayon. Coconut-like plastic buttons. **Joe Kealuhas**. $25-50

Brown tapa design with surfer. Cotton. Molded gold plastic buttons. **Royal Hawaiian**. $50-100

Surf boards and palm trees. Cotton. Coconut shell buttons. **Aloha Republic**. $50-100

"Surf-Cultural Evolution" design by Reg Mombassa, 1997. Rayon. Coconut shell buttons. **Mambo**. $75-150

Swim trunks. $50-100

A pocket cigarette lighter inscribed as a promotion for Surfrider Sportswear. *Courtesy of Dr. Gary L. Moss*

Child's shirt. $50-100

Surf riding at Waikiki Beach in the shadow of Diamondhead Point.

"Muruoa Mon Amour" design by Gerry Wedd, 1994. Made in Indonesia. Pocket label. Rayon. Coconut shell buttons. **Mambo Land Shirts**. This design was inspired by the actions of the French navy in 1994, ten years after blowing up the Greenpeace flagship, *Rainbow Warrior*, in Auckland Harbor, for resuming testing of their nuclear arsenal on the tiny Pacific atoll of Mururoa. $75-150

Surfing design. Rayon. Coconut shell buttons. **Mambo**. $75-150

Vertical surfing design. Rayon. Coconut shell buttons. **Mambo**. $75-150

All-over "Keoni" surf board, lei, and hibiscus design on cream background by John Meigs, "Keoni of Hawaii." White plastic buttons and two chest pockets with flaps. **Made in California**. *Courtesy of Dr. Gary L. Moss.* $300-500

All-over "Surfing Hawaii" design on red background. Coconut shell buttons. **Poi Pounder Tog**. *Courtesy of Dr. Gary L. Moss.* $400-600

Sepia-tone photo images of Duke Kahanamoku and team with surfboards and canoes. Coconut husk buttons. **Duke Kahanamoku An American Original.** *Courtesy of Dr. Gary L. Moss.* $100-150

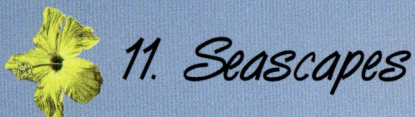
11. Seascapes

Beautiful beaches and a pounding surf create a relaxing atmosphere in Hawaii. Water sports abound and many swimming and boating activities are depicted on Hawaiian shirts. Sailing, windsurfing, and motorboats make appearances, as well as traditional outrigger canoes.

Lihue, Kauai, Hawaii, as it appeared in the 1940s.

Seascape with ocean liner. Rayon. Marbled plastic buttons. No pocket. **Presence Clothing Co. $25-50**

Seascape with ocean waves and palm trees design. Rayon. Coconut husk buttons. *Courtesy of Dr. Gary L. Moss.* $150-200

Seascape. Rayon. White plastic buttons. **Michael Gerald Ltd. Tailored in China.** $25-50

Palm trees and seascape. Rayon. Brown plastic buttons. **Pineapple Connection.** $25-50

Turbulent sea, palm trees, and bird of paradise. Rayon. Coconut shell buttons. **Tommy Bahama.** $25-50

Crepe rayon with all-over water and oval spotted fruit in blue and yellow on white ground. Coconut hull buttons in horizontal holes. **Polynesian Sportswear Hawaii.** *Courtesy of Dr. Gary L. Moss.* $100-150

Island tropical. Cotton. White inscribed buttons. **Old Navy**. $25-50

Rayon. Coconut shell buttons. **Route 66**. $25-50

Cotton. White plastic buttons. **GAP**. $25-50

Blue surf design. Rayon. Marbled plastic buttons. **Roundy Bay**. $25-50

No Problem. Jamaica. Black plastic buttons. $25-50

Blue with net fishermen and tropical design. Polyester. Made in Korea. **Royal Islander**. $25-50

Coastline. Rayon. Coconut shell buttons. **Island Fleur**. $25-50

The Outrigger Canoe Club in the 1940s.

Child's shirt. Photo print of outrigger canoe and Royal Hawaiian Hotel. **Palm Island of Miami.** *Courtesy of Dr. Gary L. Moss.* $50-100

All-over palm trees and fishing boat design on medium brown ground. No label. 1940s. *Courtesy of Dr. Gary L. Moss.* 175-250

All-over outrigger canoe and ocean design. White plastic buttons. **Pali Hawaiian Styled**. *Courtesy of Dr. Gary L. Moss*. $175-250

Seascape design with outrigger canoe. Cotton. White plastic buttons. **Evergreen Island**. $25-50

Muumuu in red seascape print with outrigger canoe. $50-100

All-over outrigger canoes in white sea on dark blue ground. Black plastic buttons in horizontal holes. **Made in California Washable.** *Courtesy Mauna Kea Gallery, Kamuela, Hawaii.* $400-600

All-over Hawaiian designs on green ground, labeled: "Royal Hawaiian," "Leis," "Outrigger Club," "Diamond Head," "Waikiki," Surfboards," "Surf and Sand," "Moana," "Sailboats." Long-sleeves and white pearl buttons in horizontal holes. Retaining the original paper button tag for Imperial Leisure Wear, with washing instructions on the reverse side, "…The Imperial Shirt Corp. Empire State Building, New York, N. Y." **Tailored by Imperial Trade Mark.** *Courtesy Mauna Kea Gallery, Kamuela, Hawaii.* $400-600

Bed sheet. Aqua beach print. Cotton flannel.

Blue fish and island design. Polyester. White plastic buttons. **Jayshire.** $25-50

The Halemaumau crater at Hawaii Volcanoes National Park, Hilo, Hawaii, as it looked in the 1940s.

Child's shirt and swim trunks. Horizontal sailboat design. Cotton. $25-50

Lighthouse. No pocket. Rayon. Marbled brown plastic buttons. **Presence Clothing Co.** $25-50

Palm trees and fish. Cotton. Marbled plastic buttons. **RJC**. $25-50

Rectangular patches of sailboat and landscape designs on medium blue background. Rayon. Black plastic buttons. **Personality**. *Courtesy of Dr. Gary L. Moss.* $100-150

Pullover shirt from a swim set in a printed design featuring water sports. (See page 81 top left.) Rayon. $150-200

Green nautical scene. Bark cloth. Cotton. White plastic buttons. **Made in Hawaii**. $50-100

Woman's silk tea-timer blouse with Japanese style all-over landscape designs on blue ground. Two hip patch pockets and gold plastic coin buttons. **Hookano brand Made in Hawaii.** *Courtesy of Dr. Gary L. Moss.* $100-150

Woman's Muumuu dress of rayon with all-over Hawaiian landscape designs on blue ground. **Made in Hawaii.** *Courtesy of Dr. Gary L. Moss.* $50-100

Blue Hawaiian design. (See also page 180 top left.) Made in Korea. Rayon. Brown plastic buttons. **Genuine Ocean Current Vintage Original Special Brand**. $50-100

All-over sailboats design on dark brown background. Rayon. White plastic buttons. **MacRoss Creation**. *Courtesy of Dr. Gary L. Moss.* $250-400

Tropical landscape. Polyester. Brown plastic buttons. **Made expressly for Harold H. Hoffer & Assoc. "The Nassau Dept." store Nassau Bahamas**. $50-100

Sailboats. Cotton. Label on pocket. White plastic buttons. **Mignot & Mignot**. $25-50.

Hat. Brown seascape design. Cotton. **Old Navy**.

Red landscape. Cotton. Wood buttons. **Paradise Found**.
$25-50

Sailing design. Placket front. Rayon. Wood buttons. **HRH**.
$25-50

Photo print of sail boats. No pocket. Long sleeves. White plastic buttons. **Joe Namath by Arrow**.
$25-50

Nautical drawing and knots with epaulettes and flap plastic. White plastic buttons. **Jantzen**.
$25-50

Swim trunks. Blue nautical design on white. (See page 95 bottom right.) **Jantzen**. $25-50

1778-1978 Discover Hawaii. Button-down collar. Cotton. White plastic buttons. **Cherokee**. $25-50

Cotton. Brown plastic buttons. **Weekender Traveler**. $25-50

Swim trunks. Drawings of ships on white background. Cotton. **Cooke Street Honolulu**. $25-50

Outrigger Canoe Club insignia. Slit pocket. Wood buttons. **HRH**. $25-50

Sailboat drawings. Made in Sri Lanka. Marbled plastic buttons. **Regatta**. $25-50

Fishing boats. Reverse side of fabric used. White plastic buttons. **AFICD Blue Water Wear**. $25-50

"The Fastnet Race." Sailing charts. Cotton. Marbled plastic buttons. **Natural Issue**. $25-50

Blue ship and floral design. Rayon. Coconut buttons. **Route 66**. $25-50

Hawaiian lighthouses design. Cotton. Brown plastic buttons. **Cooke Street Honolulu**. $25-50

Catalina Island scene. Cotton. Coconut shell buttons. **Go Barefoot**. $25-50

12. Fish

Over 650 species of fish inhabit the water surrounding the Hawaiian Islands. Many are found nowhere else in the world. Because more than half stay near the coral reefs and shore areas, fish have been both a food source and a sport item for the Hawaiian people. The following ornamental fish are commonly seen underwater while snorkeling or boating:
angel fish
blennies
butterfly fish
conger eels
moray eels
parrot fish
scorpion fish
surgeon fish
wrasses

Big-game edible fish also abound in Hawaiian waters, including:
amberjack
bonefish
goatfish
ladyfish
leatherfish
mahimahi
marlin
rainbow runner
sailfish
sea bass
snapper
swordfish
threadfish
trevally
tuna
wahoo
whales

All-over tropical fish design of red and yellow on blue water. Crepe. **Riches Honolulu**. *Courtesy of Dr. Gary L. Moss.* $250-400

All-over print of fish, plants, and starfish on yellow ground. **An authentic Hawaiian print Made in California washable.** *Courtesy of Dr. Gary L. Moss.* $400-600

Red and green all-over flying fish design. Coconut husk buttons. From the estate of Capt. Richard Kemler, this shirt was packed away in a trunk with a note reading, "I was wearing this shirt when Goddam Japs hit us at Pearl Harbor!" 1941. Very rare label: **The Wardrobe Ltd. Armed Services YMCA Honolulu, Hawaii.** *Courtesy of Dr. Gary L. Moss.* $800-1,200

All-over fish design on black background. White plastic buttons and long sleeves. **Englander Sportswear**. *Courtesy of Dr. Gary L. Moss.* $400-600

Vertical border design with fish on black background. Coconut shell buttons in vertical button holes. **Kahala Made in Hawaii.** *Courtesy of Dr. Gary L. Moss.* $800-1,200

All-over blowfish design on medium orange background with fishing nets. Rayon. Black plastic buttons. **Seawanee Sportswear**. *Courtesy of Dr. Gary L. Moss.* $400-600

All over red fish and black fishing net on white background. White plastic buttons. **Kishora by Enro**. *Courtesy of Dr. Gary L. Moss.* $175-250

All-over underwater sea life design on dark brown ground. **Made in California**. 1930-40. *Courtesy of Dr. Gary L. Moss.* $400-600

Spear fisherman design on gray background. Rayon. Coconut buttons. **Kramer's Honolulu.** *Courtesy of Dr. Gary L. Moss.* $250-400

Fish design on dark blue background. Rayon. White plastic buttons. **Royal Palm.** *Courtesy of Dr. Gary L. Moss.* $300-500

Lady's blouse with fish design on yellow background. Rayon with white plastic buttons. **Three Sisters.** *Courtesy of Dr. Gary L. Moss.* $400-600

Seahorses, fish, and seaweed design on red background. Rayon. White plastic buttons. **Cavendish.** *Courtesy of Dr. Gary L. Moss.* $400-600

Rayon with all-over flying fish design on green ground. Lettering "Flying Fish," "Hawaiian Malolo." Black plastic button in horizontal holes. **Made in California.** *Courtesy of Dr. Gary L. Moss.* $300-500

Cotton, button-down collar. Brown plastic buttons. **Bimini Bay**. $25-50

Pink fish-canning design. Silk. **Kahala**. $50-100

Cotton. Blue plastic buttons. **Appel Uniforms**. $25-50

Fish design. Cotton. Marbled plastic buttons. **Krazy Klothes Ltd.** $25-50

Woman's blouse. Fish, "island," "beach." Cotton. White plastic inscribed buttons. **Liz Claiborne Liz Wear**. $25-50

Fish design. Cotton. Brown plastic buttons. **Pacific Legend**. $25-50

Cotton. Organically sewn. White plastic buttons. **Fresh Impressions**. $25-50

Swimming trunks. *Courtesy of Dr. Gary L. Moss.* $50-100

Border print fish and flowers. Rayon. **Fun-Wear**. $25-50

White shell buttons. **Sea Island Sportswear**. $25-50

Fish. Flap pocket. Cotton. Inscribed brown plastic buttons. **Wear to Fish**. $25-50

Fish. Rayon and cotton. Marbled plastic buttons. **RJC "Made in Hawaii."** $25-50

Child's shirt with turtles design. Cotton. White plastic. **L.A. Style USA.** $25-50

Green with fish. Rayon. Dark pearly plastic buttons. **Creeks Wear**. $25-50

Net-throwing fisherman dressed in the old-style loin cloth, *malo*.

Net fishermen. Polyester. Brown plastic buttons. $25-50

Fishing. Crepe rayon. White plastic buttons. **Regular Joe USA**. $25-50

"Loud Fish 'n Chips" design in green. Rayon. Coconut shell buttons. **Mambo**. $75-100

"Loud Fish 'n Chips" design in blue. Rayon. Coconut shell buttons. **Mambo**. $75-100

Brown landscape. Cotton. Brown plastic buttons. **Peppermint Bay**. $25-50

Lahaina Whaling Spree. No pocket. Heavy cotton. White plastic buttons. **Laguna**. $50-100

Reverse fabric. Hawaiian fishing design. Cotton. White plastic buttons. **Barefoot in Paradise**. $25-50

13. Birds

A growing population in the Hawaiian Islands has caused rapid extinction of birds at an alarming rate. Of the 67 known native species, 30 are endangered and 23 have become extinct. Protected areas are stemming that trend at wildlife sanctuaries on each of the main islands. Forest dwellers and seabirds are frequently seen and have inspired many textile designers to include them in their designs. Even eagles are regularly shown. Hawaiian shirts bear witness to the great popularity of birds in Hawaii.

Japanese style eagle in clouds design on blue ground. One of the early Japanese-style shirts. **Musashiya**. *Courtesy of Dr. Gary L. Moss.* $800-1,200

Japanese style eagles and maple leaves design on dark blue ground. **Luau Sportswear**. *Courtesy of Dr. Gary L. Moss.* $200-350

All-over seagulls and clouds on a light yellow background. This is the same shirt that Harry Truman wore on the cover of *Life* magazine in December, 1951. Cream plastic buttons. **McGregor**. *Courtesy of Dr. Gary L. Moss.* $200-350

All-over white cranes and green kiwi fruit design on brown background. Rayon. White plastic buttons. **National Shirt Shops**. *Courtesy of Dr. Gary L. Moss.* $300-500

Japanese style cranes flying over the ocean design. Rayon. **Penney's**. *Courtesy of Dr. Gary L. Moss.* $150-200

Label also on back neck. Rayon. Specially marked plastic buttons. **Phat Farm**. $25-50

Slit pocket. Polyester. White plastic buttons. **Kai Nani**. $50-100

Polyester. White plastic buttons. $25-50

Red with cranes. Slit pocket. Polyester. White plastic buttons. **Kole Kole**. $25-50

Made in Japan. Eagle design. Rayon. White plastic buttons. **Penney's**. $100-150

Crane and flowers. Polyester. White plastic buttons. **Hawaiian Palm**. $25-50

Birds design. Rayon. Coconut shell buttons. **Mambo**. $75-150

Birds design. Rayon. Guess white plastic incised buttons. **Guess**. $25-50

"Seagulls" design by Bruce Goold, 1996. Rayon. Coconut shell buttons. **Mambo**. $75-150

"Currawongs" design by Bruce Goold, 1996. Rayon. Coconut shell buttons. **Mambo**. $75-150

 ## 14. Trees

Coconut palm trees and bamboo are among the most common forms of vegetation shown on Hawaiian shirts. Also *pakalolo*, the "crazy weed" in Hawaiian, is a not-so unusual plant found represented on shirts. The climate accelerates the growth of these and other plants to make them common sights on the islands. Other trees in the dynamic landscapes include the huge African tulip trees with flaming red flowers, banyans that are among the world's largest trees, and breadfruit trees that can rise over 60 feet skyward. Macadamia trees are also grown for their nuts and monkeypod trees that produce a favorite wood for woodworking.

Regal palm trees growing far inland.

All-over Hawaiian islands design with palm trees and waves in black ground. **Glentop**. *Courtesy of Dr. Gary L. Moss.* $250-400

Orange palm trees with gold outline. Cotton. Molded gold plastic buttons. **Made in Hawaii**. $50-100

Palm trees and canoe design on blue background. Rayon. White plastic buttons. **Raycrest** *Courtesy of Dr. Gary L. Moss.* $50-100

Aqua with palm trees. Cotton. Grey plastic buttons. **Union Bay**. $25-50

Black with palm trees. Rayon. Coconut shell buttons. **Java Wraps**. $25-50

Palm trees. Rayon. Marbled plastic buttons. **Paradise of the Pacific by Faulk**. $175-250

A slat-woven wall hanging painted with palm trees at a water's edge and "Aloha Hawaii." *Courtesy of Dr. Gary L. Moss.*

Black floral. Rayon. Brown plastic buttons. **Pineapple Connection**. $25-50

Vertical green palm tree rows. Cotton. No pocket. White plastic buttons. **Cutter & Buck**. $25-50

Vertical floral and palm tree rows. Cotton. Coconut shell buttons. **Old Navy**. $25-50

Dark sailing at Diamondhead design. Rayon. Wood buttons. **Original Island Sport Est. 1993**. $25-50

Swim trunks. Yellow bamboo design. Polyester and cotton. **California Rainbow by Squire of California**. $25-50

All-over colored foliage design on white background. Rayon. Marbled plastic buttons. **National Shirt Shops.**
Courtesy of Dr. Gary L. Moss. $100-150

Yellow leaves on dark blue background. Rayon. White plastic buttons. **Champion Kahanamoku.**
Courtesy of Dr. Gary L. Moss. $250-400

All-over design of stylized giraffes, cats, and leaves on grey ground. **Hampton Sportswear Hand washable.**
Courtesy of Dr. Gary L. Moss. $250-400

Vertical print of white leaves on green ground. **Kamehameha Made and styles in Hawaii for McInerny.** *Courtesy of Dr. Gary L. Moss.* $250-400

Patches of tropical scenes. Polyester. Yellow plastic buttons. **Jayshire**. $25-50

 # 15. Landscapes

Beautiful Hawaii. Each of the six main islands boasts a different sort of beauty because their landscapes are unique. Oahu has two mountain ranges that form the backdrop for Honolulu and divide the island into three distinct climates. The eastern side is lush and green with tropical plants, the center has moderate temperatures and agricultural fields, and the west is drier with an arid landscape.

Maui has two volcanoes that flowed together about a million years ago to form the only place in the world where you can climb from sea level to 10,000 feet in 38 miles. The climate ranges from tropical rainforest to arid desert.

Molokai has white beaches that fringing a desert-like landscape in the west and rainy, tropical areas in the north and east.

Lanai is small and rises quickly out of the ocean with cliffs on the west side where fantastic stone formations are strewn across the landscape.

Kauai has the wettest spot on the earth at its highest point with over 400 inches of rain annually. Just west of that spot is a collapsed volcano with "the Grand Canyon of the Pacific" that drops 3,600 feet and stretches 14 miles across.

Waterfall at Hilo, Hawaii.

All-over brown landscape design with blue waterfall at Hilo on rayon crepe. Coconut husk buttons. **Iolani**. *Courtesy of Dr. Gary L. Moss.* $175-250

Silk. Volcano crater and vertical leaf vine design. Brown plastic buttons. **Hilo Hattie**. $50-100

Green and orange floral and rainbow design. Rayon. Brown plastic buttons. **Islander**. $50-100

Horizontal landscape with beach design. Rayon. *Courtesy of Dr. Gary L. Moss.* $100-150

Crepe rayon with all-over tropical landscape design with mountains and colorful trees on blue ground. Coconut husk buttons in vertical holes. **Iolani Sportwear Hawaii.** *Courtesy of Dr. Gary L. Moss.* $175-250

Diamondhead Point at Honolulu, Oahu.

Horizontal palm tree and volcano print on white ground. White pearl buttons in horizontal holes. **Duke Champion Kahanamoku and Hawaiian original.** *Courtesy Mauna Kea Gallery, Kamuela, Hawaii.* $600-900

Souvenir tray painted with a landscape of Diamondhead Point and "Aloha Hawaii." *Courtesy of Dr. Gary L. Moss.*

Landscape on light brown background. Rayon. Coconut buttons. **Made in Hawaii.** *Courtesy of Dr. Gary L. Moss.* $100-150

Woman's wrap skirt. Diamondhead and floral design. Rayon. **Linda Bertozzi**. $25-50

Diamondhead and floral design. Rayon. White plastic inscribed Guess buttons. **Guess**. $25-50

All-over Asian landscapes with people design on dark blue background. Rayon. White plastic buttons. **Champion Kahanamoku**. *Courtesy of Dr. Gary L. Moss.* $250-400

Blue tappa and palm tree design. Made in Korea. Polyester. White plastic buttons. **Kings Road Shop/Sears**. $25-50

Rayon. Beige plastic buttons. **Color Works**. $25-50

A Hawaiian mountain trail in the 1940s.

Woman's blouse. Shoreline landscape. No pocket. Polyester. White plastic buttons. **Waltah Clarke's**. $50-100

Floral. Rayon. Purple plastic buttons. **Island Image**. $25-50

128

Volcanic crater on Hawaii, the Big Island.

Distant landscape with waterfall on black background. Rayon. **Iolani Sportswear.** *Courtesy of Dr. Gary L. Moss.* $175-250

Rayon. Green plastic buttons. **Island Image.** $25-50

Cotton. No pocket. Purple plastic buttons. **Fashion Seal Shane**. $25-50

Reproduction border print with bathing beauties. Rayon. Grey plastic buttons. **Pierre Cardin**. $25-50

Floral and framed landscapes of Hawaii. Cotton. Brown plastic buttons. **Kane Malia Made in Hawaii USA**. $25-50

Border print. Rayon. **ubc**. $25-50

Blue island and orchid design. Cotton. Brown plastic buttons. **Jade Fashions**. $25-50

Hawaiian landscapes. Polyester. Wood buttons. $25-50

All-over brown mountain landscape with palm trees design. 1950s. White plastic buttons. **Penney's**. *Courtesy of Dr. Gary L. Moss.* $50-100

 ## 16. Florals

A clothing cloth used in Polynesia and Hawaii in the nineteenth century was *pareu*. Printed cotton fabric from England that was exported to the island of Tahiti, a French territory, *pareu* usually had strong red, blue, or green backgrounds with bold, often diagonal designs of large white hibiscus or breadfruit flowers. Painter Paul Gauguin featured this sort of cloth worn as a garment by the women he depicted in the 1890s in Tahiti, and westerners took note. Sixty years later, fabric designers for Hawaiian shirt companies were influenced by Gauguin's and other artists' use of bold colors and simple floral designs.

Hawaii's plentiful sweet-smelling flowers, exotic plants, and lush vegetation make it the paradise-on-earth we know it to be. The east side of the Big Island around Hilo is the flower-growing capital of Hawaii. Here flowers for leis, including orchids, ginger, plumeria, and pikaki, are grown. Hawaiian shirts showcase a wide assortment of Hawaii's beautiful flowers and plants, including:

angel's trumpets
anthuriums
birds of paradise
bougainvillea
bromeliads
coffee
ginger in many varieties
heliconia
hibiscus
jacaranda
night-blooming cereus
orchids of many types
pandanus (*hala*)
plumeria (frangipani)
protea
silversword
taro

Vertical floral and masks. Cotton. Brown plastic buttons. **Ui-Maikai**. $50-100

Vertical floral and ukulele rows. Cotton. Brown plastic buttons. **Royal Creations**. $25-50

Pareu-inspired floral design. Slit pocket. Cotton. Molded gold plastic buttons. **Sun Dek of Hawaii**. $100-150

Red vertical floral print on yellow ground. **McGregor Made in USA**. 1950s. *Courtesy of Dr. Gary L. Moss.* $200-350

Blue "Hawaii." Rayon. White plastic buttons. **Mr. Kailua**. $50-100

Lei vendors greet tourists in the 1930s.

Hawaiian girl.

"Lei Hawaiian Style" design by John Meigs, known as Keoni of Hawaii, with black background. Rayon. Coconut husk buttons. **Kilohana.** *Courtesy of Dr. Gary L. Moss.* $500-700

Swimming trunks in the "Lei Hawaiian Style" print by John Meigs, with a red background. Rayon. **Munsingwear.** *Courtesy of Dr. Gary L. Moss.* $100-150

Aqua floral. Cotton bark cloth. Pressed silver metal buttons. **Connie's**. $25-50

Swim trunks. Ukulele and flowers on blue background. $50-100

Blue floral design. Cotton. Bark cloth. Blue plastic buttons. **Diane's Honolulu**. $50-100

Blue floral. Polyester. White plastic buttons. **Pomaré Hawaii**. $25-50

Grey floral. Rayon. White plastic buttons. **Tommy Hilfiger**. $25-50

Blue floral with gold edge. Cotton. Pressed gold metal buttons. **Made in Hawaii**. $25-50

"THC Hawaiian Textiles" selvage. White plastic buttons. **Surf Line Hawaii**. $25-50

Green floral. Cotton. Molded gold plastic buttons. **Sears Hawaiian Fashions**. $25-50

Aqua flora design. Selvage printed "Trans-Pacific Textiles." White plastic buttons. **Made in Hawaii**. $50-100

Multicolored floral design. Slit pocket. Brown plastic buttons. **Andrade**. $50-100

Green floral. Cotton. Molded gold plastic buttons. **Made in Hawaii**. $25-50

Black floral design. Slit pocket.
Black plastic buttons. **Hilo Hattie**.
$50-100

Bird of paradise on blue. Cotton.
Brown plastic buttons. **Big KNK**.
$25-50

Flowers on blue. Rayon. **Network**.
$25-50

Leaves and birds on black. Black plastic
buttons. **Hawaii Blues**. $25-50

Yellow beach scene. Cotton. Label on pocket, Original Jams. Yellow plastic buttons. **Surf Line Hawaii**. $25-50

Red leaf on blue. Polyester and rayon. **Shore Things**. $25-50

Red flowers on blue. Cotton. Blue plastic buttons. **Jantzen**. $25-50

White flowers on cotton. Marbled plastic buttons. **Box Office**. $25-50

Orchids. Rayon. Wood buttons. **Paradise Found**. $25-50

Pink and grey floral. No pocket. Rayon. White plastic buttons. **Rittenhouse Collection John Wanamaker**. $25-50

White and red floral. Cotton. **Kalaheo Styled by RJC Ltd.** **$25-50**

Floral on blue. Polyester and cotton. Blue plastic buttons. **Flair California**. $25-50

140

Blue floral. Polyester. **Live Honolulu Hawaii**. $25-50

Yellow floral. Slit pocket. Polyester. Yellow plastic buttons. **Reef Made in Hawaii**. $25-50

Red floral. Polyester and rayon. Red plastic buttons. **Shore Things**. $25-50

Selvage printed "G.V.H. Hawaii print." Polyester. Molded metal buttons. **Made in Hawaii**. $25-50

Yellow floral. Rayon. Brown plastic buttons. **Utility**. $25-50

Yellow floral design. Polyester. White plastic buttons. **Tamaré**. $25-50

Floral. Rayon. White plastic buttons. **Koko Knot**. $25-50

Souvenir Hawaiian flowers that last a lifetime.

Green floral design. White plastic buttons. **Ui Maikai**. $25-50

Child's shirt. Red floral design. Cotton. Black plastic buttons. **Made in Bangladesh**. $25-50

Orange flowers. Rayon and cotton. Molded gold plastic buttons. **Sears Hawaiian Fashions**. $25-50

Bark cloth. Cotton. Molded silver plastic buttons. **Kilii's of Hawaii**. $25-50

Red floral. Polyester and cotton. Marbled plastic buttons. **Hawaiian Tradition Brian Brothers**. $25-50

Orange floral. Polyester. White plastic buttons. **Pomaré Tahiti**. $25-50

Pink and orange. Cotton. White plastic buttons. **Liberty House**. $75-150

Vertical design of black with white flowers. Cotton. Coconut husk buttons. **Royal Hawaiian**. $75-150

Floral on black background. Cotton. Embroidery over pocket reads, "Canon." White plastic buttons. $25-50

Button-down collar. Cotton. Brown plastic buttons. $25-50

Metallic threads. Rayon and nylon. Black plastic buttons. **odo**. $25-50

Parrot design. Cotton. Wooden buttons. **Paradise Found Hawaii**. $25-50

Rayon. Brown plastic buttons. **Tori Richard**. $50-100

Vertical floral design on dark blue background. *Courtesy of Dr. Gary L. Moss.* **McGregor**. $400-600

Vertical orchids design on dark brown background. Rayon. Coconut shell buttons. **Hawaiian Surf.** *Courtesy of Dr. Gary L. Moss.* **$400-600**

All-over floral design on blue background. Rayon. Black plastic buttons. **Topflight**. $300-500

Black seaweed design on gray background. Rayon. Coconut shell buttons. **Lauhala.** *Courtesy of Dr. Gary L. Moss.* $250-400

All-over white floral design on red background. Rayon. White plastic buttons. *Courtesy of Dr. Gary L. Moss.* $175-250

All-over flower blossoms on dark green ground with yellow flowers forming a vertical border. White shell buttons in horizontal holes. **McGregor Made in U.S.A. Washable.** *Courtesy Mauna Kea Gallery, Kamuela, Hawaii.* $300-500

Vertical floral design on grey background. Rayon. Coconut shell buttons. **Shaheen's of Honolulu**. *Courtesy of Dr. Gary L. Moss.* $400-600

Flap pocket. Coconut shell buttons. **Tommy Bahama**. $25-50

Orchid design. No pocket. June 1, 1996. Trump stitching on pocket area. White plastic buttons. **Scorpio**. $50-100

Red with white blossoms, polyester slit pocket. **Tori Richard**. $50-100

Cotton. Small white plastic buttons. **Mene's**. $25-50

Polyester. White plastic buttons. **Palm Tree of Banford**. $25-50

Vertical floral design. No pocket. Brown marbled plastic buttons. **Creative Edge**. $25-50

Purple with orchids, slit pocket. Polyester. Purple plastic buttons. **Hilo Hattie**. $50-100

White flowers on green. Slit pocket. White plastic buttons. **Malihini**. $75-150

Woman's blouse. White flowers on blue. No pocket. Cotton. Pearlized blue plastic buttons. **Diane's Honolulu**. $50-100

Milticolored floral. Cotton. White plastic buttons. $25-50

Fish and leaves. Heavy cotton. **Sea Island Sportswear**. $50-100

Vertical orchids. Rayon. Wood buttons. **Paradise Found Honolulu, Hawaii**. $25-50

Woman's dress. Orange and white floral print on dark blue background. Polyester. **Royal Hawaiian**. $50-100

Orange flower on blue. Polyester. Molded silver plastic buttons with 4 Chinese characters. **Made in Hawaii**. $25-50

Silk. **Campagna Italia**. $25-50

Woman's blouse. Floral. No pocket. Rayon. Shell buttons. **Clio Petites**. $50-100

Black floral. Cotton. Marbled plastic buttons. **100% BEACH**. $25-50

All-over floral design on dark blue background. Rayon. White plastic buttons. *Courtesy of Dr. Gary L. Moss.* $300-500

Vertical floral design on dark blue background. Rayon. Long sleeves and white plastic buttons. **Mark Twain Pleasure Shirt**. *Courtesy of Dr. Gary L. Moss.* $300-500

Woman's holoku gown with vertical bird of paradise design. *Courtesy of Dr. Gary L. Moss.* $175-250

All-over pink hibiscus blossoms on white ground. **Made in Hawaii by Iolani**. *Courtesy of Dr. Gary L. Moss.* $100-150

Black vine and pod design on yellow background. Rayon. Yellow plastic buttons. *Courtesy of Dr. Gary L. Moss.* $250-400

All-over floral design on rust-red background. Brown plastic buttons. **Topflight**. *Courtesy of Dr. Gary L. Moss.* $300-500

"Flower Power" design by Jim Mitchell, 2000. Rayon. Mambo label near top of pocket. Coconut shell buttons. **Mambo.** $75-150

All-over floral print in six colors on blue ground. Coconut husk buttons in vertical holes. **Pali Hawaiian style hand print.** *Courtesy of Dr. Gary L. Moss.* $175-250

Vertical floral design on black ground. **Elbeco.** $300-500

Horizontal border print of dark pink morning glory flowers with vertical vine and leaf design up the front panels on pink ground. **Duke Champion Kahanamoku an Hawaiian original.** *Courtesy of Dr. Gary L. Moss.* $300-500

All-over floral design on black background. Rayon. White plastic buttons. *Courtesy of Dr. Gary L. Moss.* $250-400

All-over design of gray and yellow leaves on a brown thatched background. Brown plastic buttons. **Car-lette Sportswear**. *Courtesy of Dr. Gary L. Moss.* $150-200

Purple and blue all-over floral design on cotton bark cloth. Purple plastic buttons. **Made in Hawaii for Marjy Stevens Hawaiian Shops**. *Courtesy of Dr. Gary L. Moss.* $100-150

All-over flowers design on a dark blue background. White plastic buttons. **Andover**. *Courtesy of Dr. Gary L. Moss.* $175-250

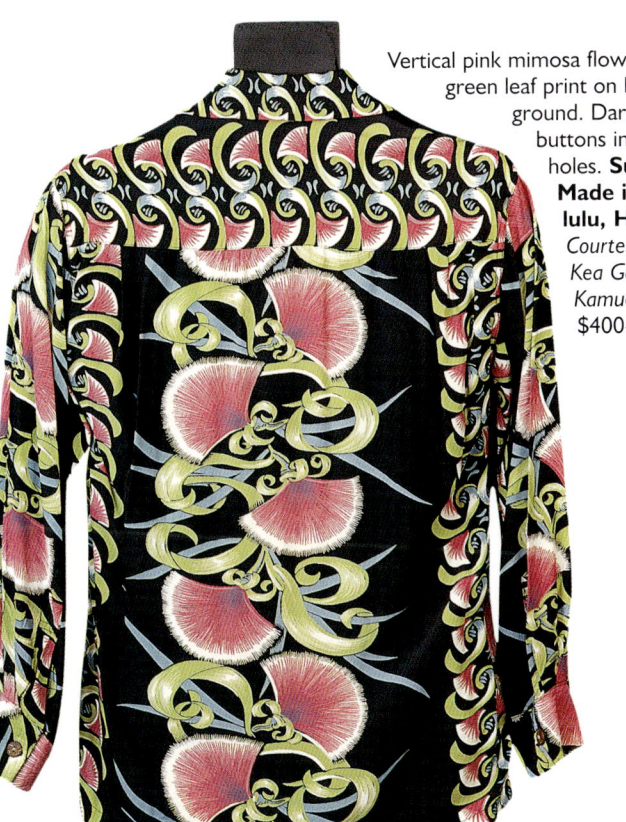

Vertical pink mimosa flowers and green leaf print on black ground. Dark coconut buttons in horizontal holes. **Surf'n Sand Made in Honolulu, Hawaii.** *Courtesy Mauna Kea Gallery, Kamuela, Hawaii.* $400-600

Vertical white leaf and helmeted head print on black ground. Dark coconut buttons in vertical holes. **Paradise Sportswear Made in Hawaii.** *Courtesy Mauna Kea Gallery, Kamuela, Hawaii.* $600-900

All-over leaf design on green background. Rayon. Two chest pockets and coconut shell buttons. **Coopers Sport Shirt.** *Courtesy of Dr. Gary L. Moss.* $300-500

Blue with floral design. Cotton. Coconut shell buttons. **HRH**. $25-50

Woman's *pake muu*. Vertical floral design on brown background. *Courtesy of Dr. Gary L. Moss.* $150-200

Vertical leaf and floral design on black ground. Black plastic buttons in horizontal holes. **Kamehameha made and styled in Hawaii.** *Courtesy Mauna Kea Gallery, Kamuela, Hawaii.* $600-900

Leaves on a grey background. Cotton. Coconut buttons. **Tommy Bahama**. $25-50

Shirt and matching swim trunks. Red floral design on blue. Blue plastic buttons. Cotton. **Dr. Beach**. $25-50 each

Woman's *pake muu*. All-over floral and leaf design. *Courtesy of Dr. Gary L. Moss.* $100-150

Swim trunks. Yellow trellis and orange floral design. Cotton. **Jantzen**. $25-50

Swim trunks. Red floral design. Cotton. $25-50

Swim trunks. Orange leaf design with grey knit panels. *Courtesy of Dr. Gary L. Moss.* $50-100

Swim trunks. Red and green floral design. Cotton. $25-50

Swim trunks. Vertical white floral design on dark blue background. *Courtesy of Dr. Gary L. Moss.* $50-100

Swim trunks. Vertical floral design. *Courtesy of Dr. Gary L. Moss.* $75-150

Swim trunks. Blue and white floral. Cotton. Coconut shell buttons. **Duke Kahanamoku by Catalina**. $25-50

Green floral. Rayon. Brown plastic buttons. **Pazzo**. $25-50

"Frangipani #1" design by Bruce Goold, 1995. Rayon. Mambo label on corner of pocket. Coconut shell buttons. **Mambo Classic Rayon**. $75-150

Pink floral design. Cotton. White plastic buttons. **Hawaiian Casuals**. $25-50

Shaded white floral design. Cotton. Plastic incised "Ralph Lauren Chaps" buttons. **Ralph Lauren Chaps**. $25-50

Made in Romania. Rayon. Red plastic buttons. **Bouvy**. $25-50

Slit pocket. Polyester. Cloth-covered buttons. **Pacific Isle Creations**. $25-50

Floral. Polyester and cotton. Green plastic buttons. **Haband of Paterson**. $25-50

Cotton. Red plastic buttons. $25-50

Flowers on blue. Rayon. Blue plastic buttons. **Bouvy Paris New York**. $25-50

Flowers on blue. Rayon. Wood buttons. **Paradise Found**. $25-50

Floral. Rayon. Blue/green plastic buttons. **Island Image**. $25-50

Aqua and white floral design. Made in Honolulu. Polyester and cotton. Pressed silver metal buttons. **Paradise Hawaii**. $25-50

Blue vertical floral rows. Cotton. Long sleeves. **Mach II by Arrow**. $25-50

Floral and skeleton design. Rayon. Coconut shell buttons. **Mambo**. $75-150

Floral design. Rayon. Coconut shell buttons. **Mambo**. $75-150

Red roses design. Rayon. Coconut shell buttons. **Mambo**. $75-150

"Hyperbiscus" floral design by Stephen Bliss, 1996. Rayon. Coconut shell buttons. **Mambo**. $75-150

Flowers and cars design. Rayon. Coconut shell buttons. **Mambo**. $75-150

Leaves design. Rayon. Coconut shell buttons. **Mambo**. $75-150

Floral design. Rayon. Coconut shell buttons. **Mambo**. $75-150

Scattered islands with people on a speckled brown background. Rayon. White plastic buttons. **Champion Kahanamoku.** *Courtesy of Dr. Gary L. Moss.* $200-350

Woman's Muumuu dress of rayon with all-over sailboats and Hawaiian floral designs on brown ground. **Made in Hawaii.** $50-100

Swim trunks. Tropical plants design. Grey plastic button. $25-50

17. Food & Drink

Poi, or mashed taro root, is the traditional staple food in Hawaii. "He who says he likes poi is either a Hawaiian or a liar." (Old saying.) Hawaii is among the largest sugar-producing areas in the United States. Ancient Hawaiians knew sugar cane was an energy source for long canoe voyages. The principal fruits grown in Hawaii include breadfruit, coconut, avocado, guava, pineapple, papaya, macadamia nuts, mango, banana, kiwi, and litchi. With 325,000 acres in grazing lands, the privately owned Parker Ranch on the Big Island qualifies as the largest Hereford beef cattle ranch in the world. Kona coffee is grown on the Big Island and several Hawaiian vineyards produce local wines.

Hawaiian fruits.

Enyce Von Coco cocktail. Coconut design. Rayon and cotton. Brown plastic buttons. **Enyce**. $25-50

Brown coconut and white palm frond design on dark blue background. Rayon. Coconut husk buttons. **Robin Hood Sportswear.** *Courtesy of Dr. Gary L. Moss.* $250-400

"Coconutters" design by Jim Mitchell, 1999. Rayon. Pearl plastic buttons. **Mambo**. $75-150

Gourds design on dark blue background. Rayon. Coconut shell buttons. **H.A. & E. Smith Bermuda Made in Hawaii**. *Courtesy of Dr. Gary L. Moss.* $400-600

Papaya fruit tree.

Banana bunch and hibiscus design on burgundy background. Coconut shell buttons. **It's Levi Strauss**. *Courtesy of Dr. Gary L. Moss.* $175-300

Rayon with all-over banana fruit and leaf design on white ground. Swimsuit shirt with two hip patch pockets and no breast pocket. White shell buttons in horizontal holes. **Ceeb of Miami Miami Sportswear Co.** *Courtesy of Dr. Gary L. Moss.* $75-150

Cotton. Blue plastic buttons. **Made in Hawaii.** $25-50

Pineapple design on green background. Long sleeves and coconut shell buttons. **Made in Hawaii.** *Courtesy of Dr. Gary L. Moss.* $500-700

All-over pineapples and leaves on a light yellow background. Rayon. Yellow plastic buttons. Two chest pockets with flaps. **Florida Sunwear Inc. Miami**. *Courtesy of Dr. Gary L. Moss.* $150-200

All-over pineapples and palm trees on a dark blue background. Rayon. White plastic buttons. **Mylan**. *Courtesy of Dr. Gary L. Moss.* $200-350

Pineapples on light blue background. Rayon with two chest pockets with flaps and long sleeves. White plastic buttons. **Random Wear.** *Courtesy of Dr. Gary L. Moss.* **$200-350**

Child's shirt. Pineapple on shaded orange background. Cotton. Molded gold plastic buttons. **Made in Hawaii**. $25-50

Red pineapples and palm trees design on green background. Rayon. White plastic buttons. **National Shirt Shops**. *Courtesy of Dr. Gary L. Moss.* $150-200

Pineapples. No pocket. Rayon. Grey plastic buttons. **INC International Concepts**. $25-50

White flowers on black. Rayon. Brown plastic buttons. **White Oak**. $25-50

Red with palm trees. Cotton. Red plastic buttons. **Islander**. $25-50

Vertical ship and pineapples rows. Polyester and cotton. Shell buttons. $25-50

Orange bark cloth. Slit pocket. Molded gold plastic button with four characters. **Diamondhead Sportswear**. $50-100

Kona Coffee. Polyester. White plastic buttons. **Royal Palm Hawaii**. $50-100

Cotton. Sushi food items. Coconut shell buttons. **Locals Only**. $25-50

Primo beer design. Heavy cotton. Metallic over plastic buttons with inscribed Aloha Hawaii. $50-100

Primio beer design. Bark cloth. Cotton. Gold plastic buttons with pattern. **Ui Maikai**. $50-100

Cocktails/wine. Rayon. Coconut husk buttons. **Cherokee Waikiki Wear**. $25-50

Primo Hawaiian beer design. Cotton. Coconut shell buttons. **Go Barefoot**. $50-100

18. Tourism

Polynesian people have been discovering Hawaii's finest features for over a thousand years; Europeans for a mere three hundred. The first Japanese workers came to Hawaii in 1868, and more from Portugal arrived in 1878.

In the early twentieth century, cruise ships from America brought visitors on a 6-day journey that made the Hawaiian Islands practically accessible for the first time. From the 1920s to the 1940s, the Aloha Tower marketplace at the ship's harbor in Honolulu was a center of tourism. Cruise ships docked across the harbor and the famous clock tower was a landmark and the tallest structure in the city.

But tourism in Hawaii got a huge boost on April 17, 1935, when Pan Am World Airways flew its first China Clipper airship from the west coast of the United States to Honolulu in 18 hours. TWA, United, Northwest Orient, and many other airlines soon followed. Today, tourism is the number one industry in the state.

The *SS Lurline* arrives in Honolulu harbor near the Aloha Tower in the 1940s.

Lurline ship design. Silk. Coconut shell buttons. **Avanti**. $50-100

Ocean liner landing. Brown plastic buttons. **Utility**. $25-50

A passenger with leis on the deck of a cruise ship awaits embarkation at Honalulu.

A souvenir cigarette case enameled with the Clipper airship over Hawaiian palm trees.

Northwest Orient Airlines advertising brochure for Hawaii.

American Hawaii Cruises design showing the ships *Independence* and *Constitution*. Polyester and cotton. White plastic buttons. **Hans Jütte for American Hawaii Cruises**. $50-100

Two-piece rayon woman's pajamas with travel insignia for United Air Lines, Santa Fe railroad, American Airlines, Fly TWA, Delta airlines, United States Lines, Sun Valley Idaho, PAA, and drawings of ocean liners, trains, and airplanes on dark blue ground. White plastic buttons in vertical holes. *Courtesy of Dr. Gary L. Moss.* $75-150

Pontoon aircraft design. Cotton. Black plastic buttons. **Yo Wear USA.** (Boxer dog face). $25-50

Swim trunks. Groups of tourists and Hawaiians on blue background. Cotton. **GAP.** $25-50

Tourists and sea planes. Rayon. Coconut shell buttons. **Reyn Spooner**. $50-100

Hawaiian words postcards. Silk. Multicolor plastic buttons. **Peter Et Jon.** $25-50

Camera, postcard, and stamp border print. Cotton and rayon. Marbled plastic buttons. **Arizona**. $25-50

Waikiki Wedding and *Hawaiian Nights* music covers. Cotton. White plastic buttons. **Accents by Berné**. $25-50

White with drawn landscape. "Pacific Ocean." **Ocean Pacific**. $25-50

Picture print of scenes in Honolulu on white ground. White plastic buttons in horizontal holes. **Towncraft**. *Courtesy Mauna Kea Gallery, Kamuela, Hawaii.* $400-600

Postcards design on blue. Rayon. Coconut shell buttons. **Utility**. $25-50

Postcards design on brown. Rayon. Marbled plastic buttons. **M. E. Sport**. $25-50

Cartoon-style labeled pictures on yellow patterned ground. Cotton. Coconut shell buttons. **Go Barefoot**. $25-50

Seersucker cloth with eight photo images of tourists in the Hawaiian Islands interspersed with propeller-driven airplanes on a red background, late 1940s. *Courtesy of Dr. Gary L. Moss.*

Blue Hawaiian labels, stamp. Modern Sultanate of Oman. Cotton and rayon. Brown molded plastic buttons. **Cactus Black Label.** $25-50

Surf boards and travel posters. No pocket. Polyester. Brown plastic buttons. **K.A.D. Clothing** $25-50

Tropical coast line. Rayon. Marbled plastic buttons. **Bi Bay Sports**.

Blue Hawaiian design. (See also page 93 bottm right) Made in Russia. Rayon. Brown plastic buttons. **Pineapple Connection**. $25-50

Aloha Tower at Honolulu design, with sailboats. Green plastic buttons. **Original by Hale Hawaii**. *Courtesy of Dr. Gary L. Moss.* $250-400

Honolulu's Aloha Tower. Rayon. Marbled plastic buttons. **Tribes**. $25-50

Blue Hawaiian scenes. Cotton. Molded silver plastic buttons with four Asian symbols. $25-50

Green vertical floral. Pressed metal buttons. **Fashions of Hawaii**. $50-100

Hawaiian scenes. Cotton. Coconut shell buttons. **Old Navy**. $25-50

Woman's shirt. Silk. Black plastic buttons. **Robert Stock**. $25-50

19. Advertising

The colorful potential of well designed graphics to get across a message is not lost on the manufacturers of Hawaiian shirts. Special designs to advertise products, companies, and organizations appear on Hawaiian shirts in subtle as well as direct images. Sometimes these shirts are made for participants of conventions and gala functions, to both set these people apart and to unite them into a group. They become souvenirs and keepsakes, and commemorate the events in a clever and useful way.

Red stylized tapa design on white background incorporating McDonald's restaurant insignia arches and "Hawaii 71." Produced for the 1971 McDonald's convention. White plastic buttons. *Courtesy of Dr. Gary L. Moss.* $50-100

All-over "United Airlines" design on light brown background. Limited edition shirt made in 1952 for United Airlines' inaugural flight to Hawaii. "Nellie McGuire welcomes you." Coconut husk buttons. **Surfriders**. *Courtesy of Dr. Gary L. Moss.* $800-1,200

All-over white "Maytag" design on red background. Cotton. Coconut shell buttons. **Sun Fashions of Hawaii**. *Courtesy of Dr. Gary L. Moss.* $100-150

Fez and scimitar design on white background. Cotton with brown plastic buttons. **Alfred Shaheen Honolulu**. *Courtesy of Dr. Gary L. Moss.* $175-250

NR Hawaii 1979 design. Slit pocket. Cotton & polyester. Clear plastic buttons with white rim. $25-50

Blue Elk's Club insignia and stylized tapa design on white background. White plastic buttons. This shirt was made in 1971 for the California-Hawaii Elks State Association convention in Honolulu. **Hawaiian Incentives Services.** *Courtesy of Dr. Gary L. Moss.* $50-100

All-over inscribed rectangles on light yellow ground. Orange, pink, and green details. **Made in Hawaii**. 1960s. *Courtesy of Dr. Gary L. Moss.* $100-150

"Cootie" game design. © 2001 Hasbro Inc.. No pocket. Cotton. Blue plastic buttons. **Cootie Brand**. $25-50

Side Pocket and other pool halls in Honolulu. Polyester. Dark blue inscribed Koman buttons. **Koman**. $25-50

No pocket. Cotton. Just Born, Inc. c. 2001. Black plastic buttons. **Hot Tamales**. $25-50

Horizontal "surf summer" design with beer bottles and beach scenes. Cotton. **Nicole Miller**. $25-50

Gift certificate card for Trader Joe stores, printed paper, 2004.

20. Shirt Details

Details of a Hawaiian shirt's construction and condition can help to determine its age and authenticity.

Faded flap pockets and a lack of fading beneath the flap are apparent on old shirts worn in the sunshine.

The outside and the inside surfaces of well printed rayon fabric look almost identical.

Double stitching on the shoulder seam indicates good, firm construction found on older shirts.

Fading under the collar is apparent on old shirts that have been worn in the sunshine.

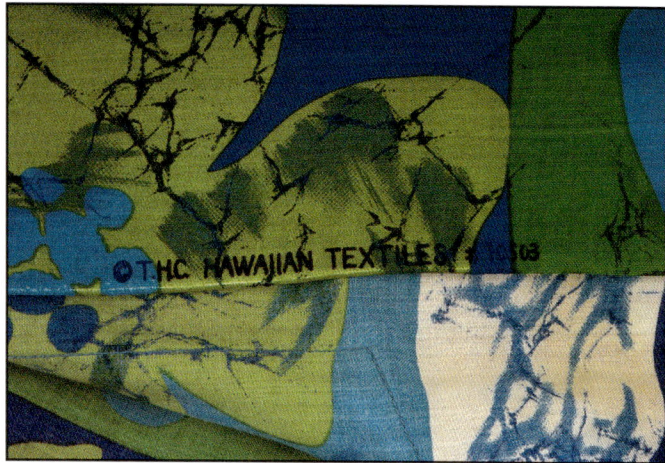

A selvage printed with the manufacturer's name.

A closely matched patch pocket.

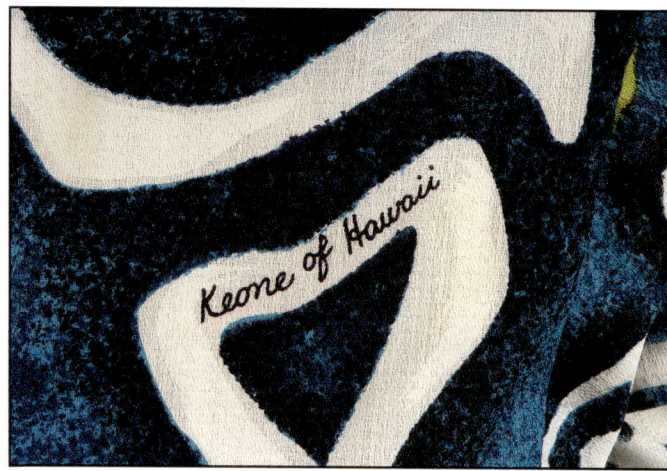

A designer's signature in the design.

A flap pocket.

A perfectly matched patch pocket.

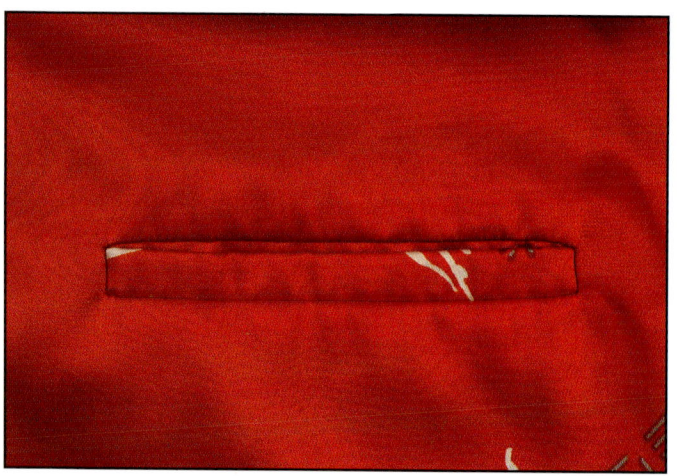

A slit pocket.

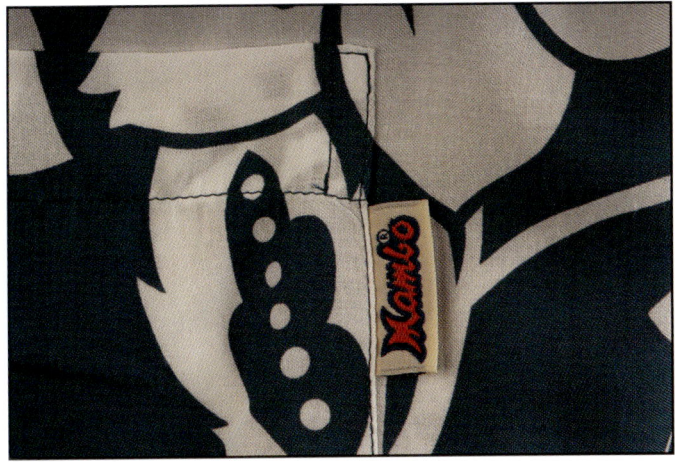
Manufacturer's label on a pocket.

Vertical button hole and regular, round, coconut shell button.

Manufacturer's label on a pocket.

Horizontal button holes may indicate a pre-1960 manufacture.

Seahorse-shaped coconut button.

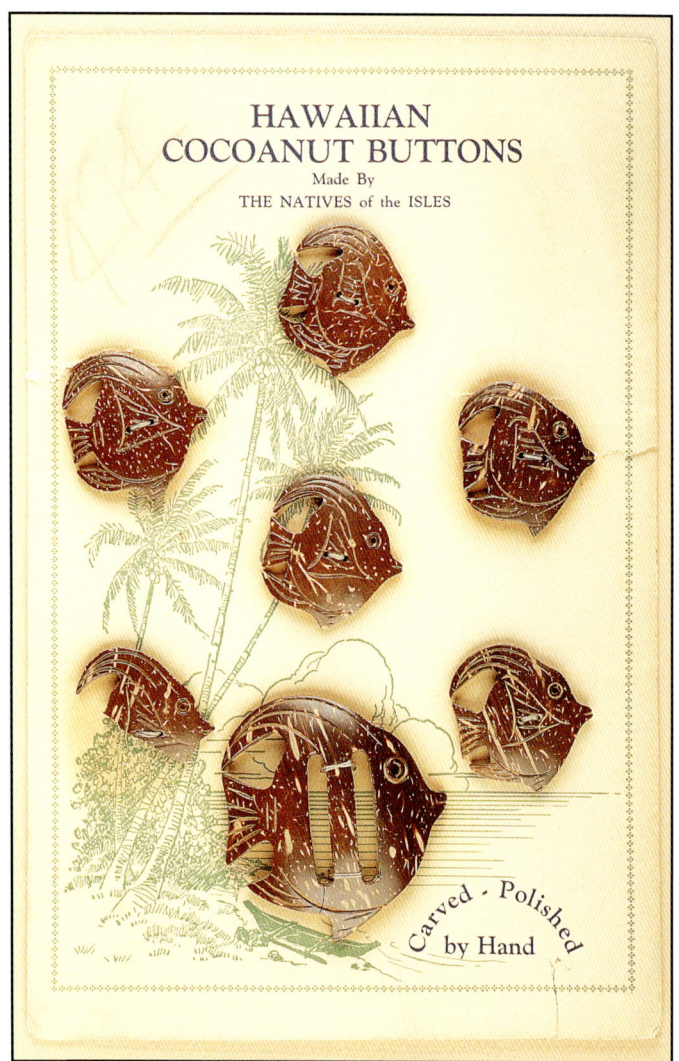

Coconut husk button.

White plastic button.

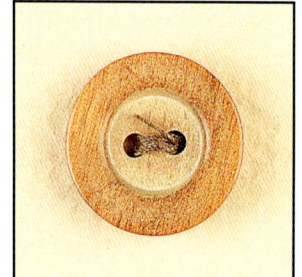

Wooden button.

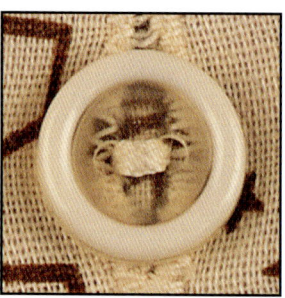

Clear plastic button with white rim.

White plastic button.

Multicolored plastic button.

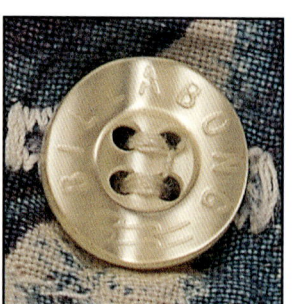

Billabong inscribed button.

Fish-shaped coconut buttons.

Small clamshell button.

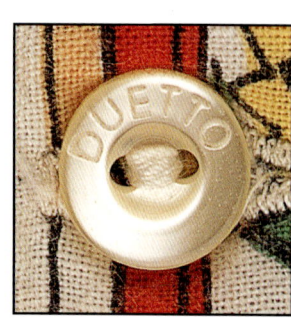

Duetto inscribed button.

Esprit Sport inscribed button.

Koman inscribed button.

Liz Wear inscribed button.

Old Navy inscribed button.

Phat Farm inscribed button.

Ralph Lauren Chaps inscribed button.

Wear to Fish inscribed button.

Molded gold plastic button.

Silver plastic button.

Metal over white plastic button.

Gold plastic button.

Thin metal inscribed "Aloha Hawaii" over plastic button.

Metal griffin button.

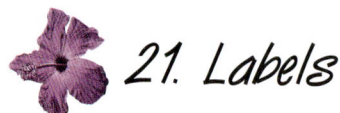 21. Labels

Manufacturer's and retail labels on Hawaiian shirts have become interesting collectibles in their own right. They can help to date and identify the origins of the shirts and textile designs on which they appear, and they possess their own graphic styles as well. The following labels all have been found on the Hawaiian shirts studied for this book.

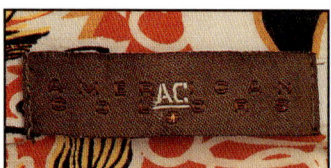
AC

Aloha Republic

Andrade

Bai Nani

Accents

American Archives

Andrade

Banana Jack

Address Unknown

American Blue

Arizona

Bar Code

Alfred Shaheen

Andover

Avanti

B-Boyz

Aloha Kanaka

Andrade

Bahama Paradise

Beach

Bear Creek

Bog

Bullock & Jones

California

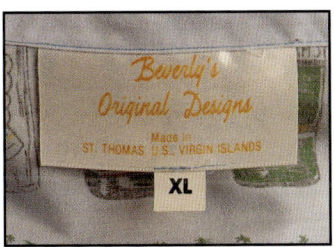
Beverly's Original Designs

Bouvy

Bush Pilot

California

Billabong

Box Office

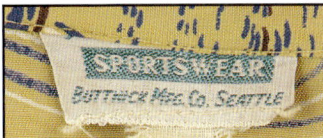
Buttrick

California

Billion Bay

Box Office

B.V.D.

California

Bimini Bay

Brass Buckle

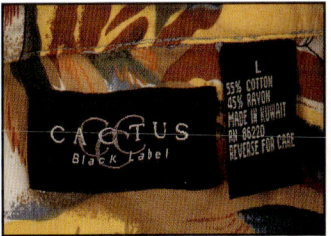
Cactus Black Label

Campagnia Italia

Blue Water Wear

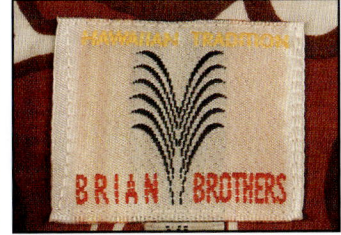
Brian Brothers

Calabash

Campia Moda

 Canon	 Chaps	 Cooke Street	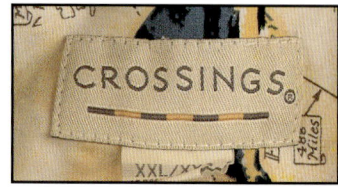 Crossings
 Canopy	 Cherokee	 Coopers	 Desmond's
 Car-Lette	 Cherokee	 Coopers	 Diamondhead Sportswear
 Catalina	 CLIO	 Cootie	 Diane's
 Cavendish	 Club	 Creative Edge	 Double Impact
 Ceeb	 Connie's	 Cross Colors	 Dragonfly

Duetto

Englander

First Down

Glentop

Duke Champion Kahanamoku

Enyce

Fivecrown

Go Barefoot

Duke Champion Kahanamoku

Esprit

Flair

Gotcha Sport

Duke Champion Kahanamoku

Evergreen Island

Florida Sunwear

Guess

Duke Kahanamoku

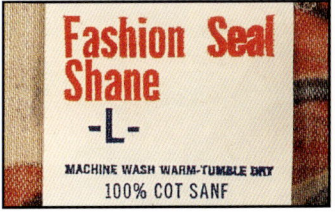
Fashion Seal Shane

Fresh Impressions

Haband of Paterson

Elbeco

Fashions of Hawaii

Gap

Haggar Clothing

Hale Hawaii

Hawaiian Casuals

Hawaiian Surf

Hookano

Hale Hawaii

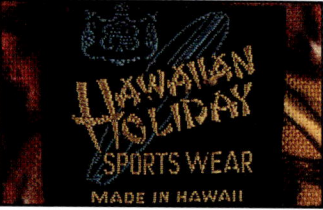
Hawaiian Holiday

Helen's

Hookano Brand

Hale Hawaii

Hawaiian Incentive Services

Hoaloha

Hot Tamales

Hampton Sportswear

Hawaiian Original

Holiday Sportswear

Howie

Hans Jütte

Hawaiian Palm

Honalulu Hawaii

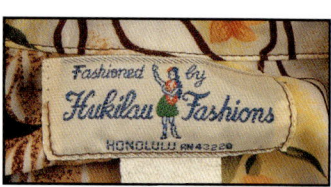
Hukilau Fashions

Harper

Hookano

HRH

 Hukilau Fashions
 INC International Concepts
 Island Image
 Jantzen

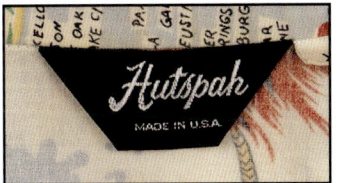 Hutspah
 Iolani
 Island Image
 Jantzen

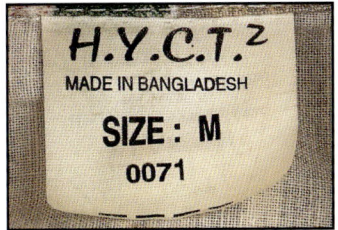 H.Y.C.T.
 Iolani
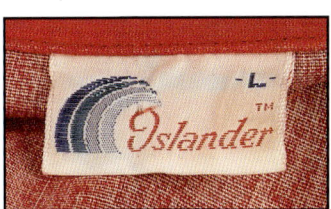 Islander
 Japanese Bazaar

 Iceberg
 Iolani
 Jade Fashions
 Java Wraps

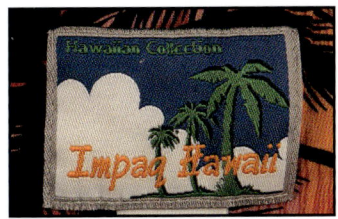 Impaq Hawaii
 Island Creations
 Jahaca Prints
 Jayshire

 Imperial
 Island Fever Jams World
 J.J. Cochran

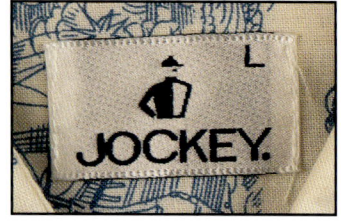
Jockey

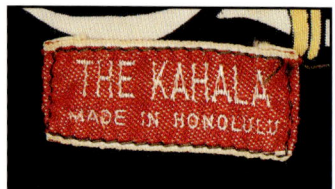
Kahala

Kahili

Kanoi Koi

Joe Kealuhas

Kahala

Kai Nani

Kapito

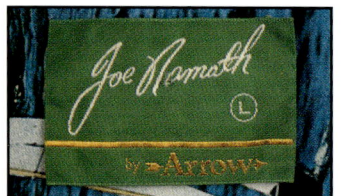
Joe Namath

Kahala

Kalaheo

Ke Nui

Jolen

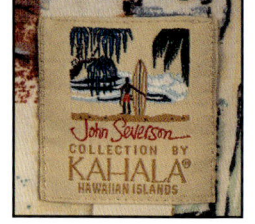
Kahala

Kamehameha

Kennington

K.A.D. Clothing Co.

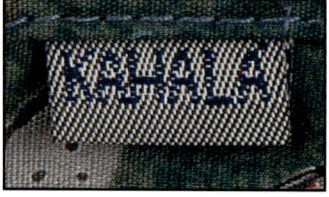
Kahala

Kamehameha

Khaki Safau

K.A.D. Clothing

Kahana Manufacturing Company

Kane Malia

King Size

Kings Road

Kona Kai

Kuu Ipo

Levi Straus

Kishora

Kramer's

L.A. Style

Le Tigre

Kole Kole

Krazy Klothes

Laguna

Liberty House

Koman

Krush Hawaii

Laguna

Liberty House

Kona Kai

Kulani Beach

Lauhala

Life's A Beach

Kona Kai

Kuonakakai

Leilani

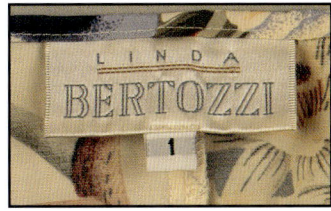
Linda Bertozzi

Liz Claiborne

MacRoss Creation

Made in Hawaii

Mambo

Locals Only

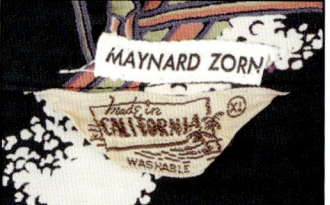
Made in California

Made in Japan

Mambo

Luau Sportswear

Made in Hawaii

Malibo

Mambo

Mach II

Made in Hawaii

Malihini

Manhattan

Machin

Made in Hawaii

Mambo

Marc Edwards

Machin Shirtmaker

Made in Hawaii

Mambo

Marc Edwards

Margenata | McGregor | Mitford | Musashiya

Marjy Stevens | M.E. Sport | Modesto | Mylan

Mark Twain | M.E. Sport | Montage Tropics | Napili

McGregor | The Men's Store | Monticerutti | National

 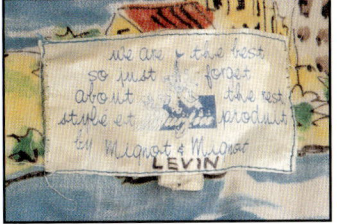  

McGregor | Mignot & Mignot | Morro Bay | National

 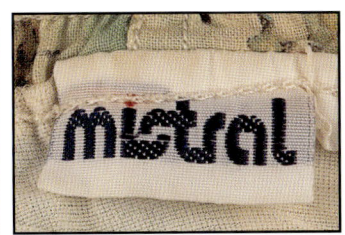  

McGregor | Mistral | Mukai Fashions | National

Natural Issue

No Dice

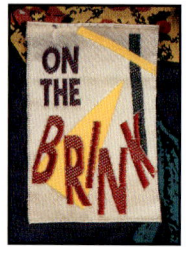
On the Brink

Pali

Nautica

Nui Nalu

OP

Pali

NEWS

Ocean Current

Orchid Fashions

Paradise Blue Lagoon

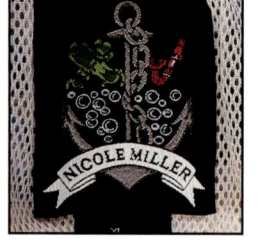
Nichole Miller

odo

Original Island Sport

Paradise Found

NLMT

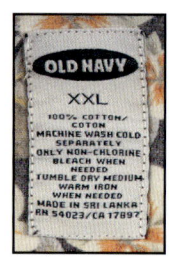
Old Navy

Pacific Isle Creations

Paradise Found

No Boundaries

Onita

Pacific Legend

Paradise of the Pacific

Paradise Sportwear

Pennleigh

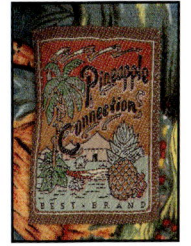
Pineapple Connection

Pride

Paul Smith

Peppermint Bay

Pineapple Connection

Random Wear

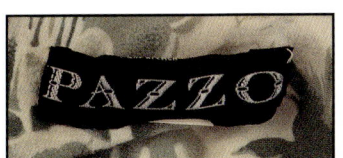
Pazzo

Personality

Poi Pounder Tog

Raycrest

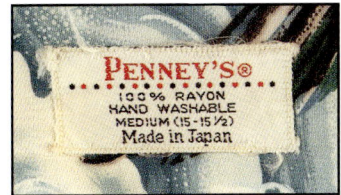
Penney's

Peter Et Jon.

Polyneisan

Reef

Penney's

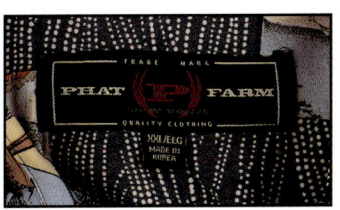
Phat Farm

Pomaré Tahiti

Regular Joe

Penney's

Pierre Cardin

Presence

Repáge

 Reyn Spooner
 Robert Graham
 Royal Creations
 Royal Palm

 Reyn Sportswear
 Robin Hood
 Royal Hawaiian
 Royal Palm

 Richard Douglas
 Ross Sutherland
 Royal Hawaiian
 Rusty

 Riches
 Ross Sutherland
 Royal Hawaiian
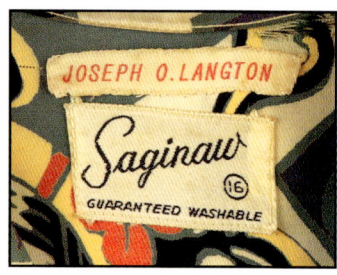 Saginaw

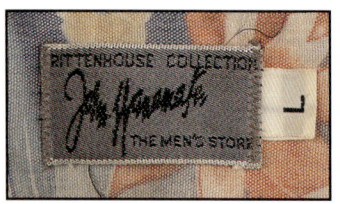 Rittenhouse Collection
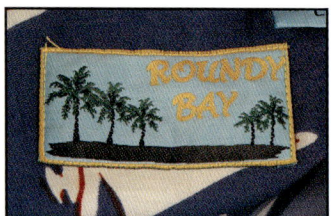 Roundy Bay
 Royal Islander
 Scorpio

 R.J.C.
 Route 66
 Royal Hawaiian
 Sea Island

Sea Island

Shore Things

Substudio

Surfriders Sportswear

Sears

Shoreline Hawaii

Sun Fashions

Taboo

Sears

Silk Club

Sun Fashions of Hawaii

Tamare

Sergio Valente

Silk Club

Surf-In by Mignot n Mignot

Tapa Design

Seawanee

SR. Clifford Holiday Wear

Surf Line Hawaii

Terrace Club

Shaheen's

Styled for County Road

Surf 'N Sand

Three Sisters

Thums Up For Him

Towncraft

Tropicana

Ui-Maikai

Tina Fashions

Towncraft

Tropicana

Ui-Maikai

Tommy Bahama

Trans-Pacific Textiles

Tropicana

Ui-Maikai

Topflight

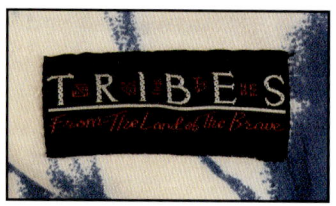
Tribes

Tropicool

Union Bay

Tori Richard

Tropical Fashions

Trust

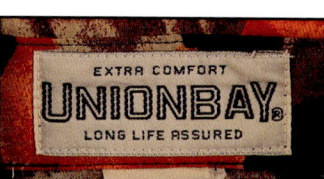
Union Bay

Tori Richard

Tropicana

ubc

Utility

   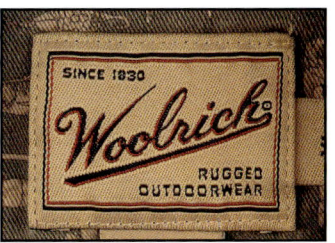

| Waltah Clarke's | Watumull's | Westwood Casuals | Woolrich |

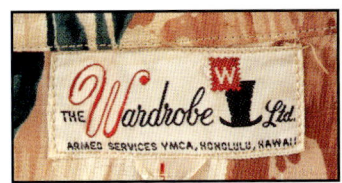    

| The Wardrobe Ltd. | Wave by Scorpio Products | Wheatley | | Yo Wear |

 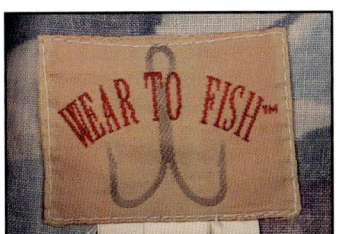  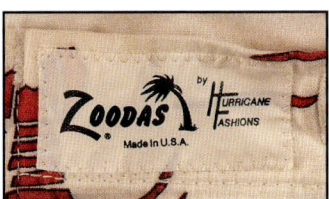

| Watumull's | Wear to Fish | Windswept | Zoodas |

Recommended Reading

Blackburn, Mark. *Hawaiiana, The Best of Hawaiian Design*. Atglen, Pennsylvania: Schiffer Publishing Ltd., 1996.

Congdon-Martin, Douglas in cooperation with the California Heritage Museum, Santa Monica, California. *Aloha Spirit, Hawaiian Art & Popular Design*. Atglen, Pennsylvania: Schiffer Publishing Ltd., 1996.

Golding, Wayne. *Still Life With Franchise*. Rushcutters Bay, New South Wales: Mambo Graphics Pty., Ltd., 1998.

Hope, Dale, with Gregory Tozian. *The Aloha Shirt, Spirit of the Islands*. Hillsboro, Oregon: Beyond Words Publishing, Inc., 2000.

Master Book of Hawaiian Shirt. Japan: World Photo Press, 2000.

Master Book of Hawaiian Shirt 2, Aloha Style Presented by Sun Surf. Japan: World Photo Press, 2002.

Schiffer, Nancy N. *Hawaiian Shirt Designs*. Atglen, Pennsylvania: Schiffer Publishing, Ltd., 1997.

_____. *Tripocal Shirts & Clothing*, Atglen, Pennsylvania: Schiffer Publishing, Ltd., 1998.

Steele, H. Thomas. *The Hawaiian Shirt, Its Art and History*. New York: Abbeville Press, 1984.

Hula

Index

AAA Travel, 9
AC, 190
Accents by Berné, 177, 190
Address Unknown, 51, 190
Adolfo, 65
Alfred Shaheen, 148, 183, 190
Aloha Kanaka, 73, 190
Aloha Republic, 80, 190
American Archives, 56, 190
American Blue, 79, 190
American Colors, 42
American Hawaiian Cruises, 194
Andover, 156, 190
Andrade, 26, 42, 77, 137, 190
Apple Uniforms, 103
Arizona, 77, 190
Arrow, 95
Artvogue, 73
Avanti, 174, 190

Bahama Paradise, 190
Bai Nani, 33, 190
Banana Jack, 190
Bar Code, 190
Barefoot in Paradise, 27, 109
B-Boyz, 190
Beach, 190
Bear Creek, 191
Beverly's Original Designs, 191
Bi Bay Sports, 179
Big KNK, 138
Billabong, 10, 191
Billion Bay, 103, 191
BJ Bay Sports, 49
Bimini Bay, 103, 191
Blue Angel Fish Tropical Water Beauties, 8
Blue Water Wear, 97, 191
Bog, 191
Bouvy, 162, 163, 191
Box Office, 72, 139, 191
Brass Buckle, 191
Brian Brothers, 144, 191
Bruno, 74
Bullock & Jones, 75, 191
Bun Fashions, 71
Bush Pilot, 191
Buttons, 187-189
Buttrick, 191
B.V.D., 71, 191

Cactus Black Label, 179, 191
Calabash, 50, 191
California, 119, 191
Campagnia Italia, 152, 191
Campia Moda, 2, 71, 191
Campus, 60
Canon, 192
Canopy, 192
Car-Lette, 156, 192

Catalina, 24, 25, 36, 160, 192
Cavendish, 102, 192
Ceeb, 169, 192
Champion, 34, 35, 55, 58, 119, 124, 126, 155, 166, 193
Chaps, 67, 161, 192
Cherokee, 96, 173, 192
Chun, Ellery, 37
Cisco, 35
CLIO, 41, 152, 192
Club, 34, 192
Code Sheet, 54
Color Works, 126
Connie's, 135, 192
Cook, Capt. Jas., 17
Cooke Street, 96, 98, 192
Coopers, 29, 157, 192
Cootie, 184, 192
Creeks Wear, 106
Creative Edge, 20, 149, 192
Cross Colors, 192
Crossings, 192
Cut Off Creek, 33
Cutter & Buck, 118

Desmond's, 192
D.F. Clothing Co., 41
Diamondhead Sportswear, 172, 192
Diane's, 135, 150, 192
Double Impact, 192
Dragonfly, 41, 192
Dr. Beach, 159
Duetto, 193
Duke Champion Kahanamoku, 24, 25, 83, 124, 155, 160, 193

Elbeco, 155, 193
Englander, 100, 193
Enro, 101
Enyce, 167, 193
Esprit, 193
Evergreen Island, 89, 193

Fashion Seal Shane, 130, 193
Fashions of Hawaii, 181, 193
Faulk, 117
First Down, 54, 193
Fivecrown, 193
Flair, 140, 193
Florida Sunwear, 169, 193
Fresh Impressions, 104, 193
Fun-Wear, 105

Gap, 59, 86, 176, 193
Gaugain, Paul, 5
Glentop, 115, 193
Go Barefoot, 98, 173, 178, 193
Gotcha Sport, 193
Guess, 113, 125, 193

Haband of Paterson, 162, 193
H.A. & E. Smith, 168
Haggar Clothing, 193
Hakihu Fashion, 71
Haleakala, 5
Hale Hawaii, 18, 47, 61, 180, 194
Hallmark, 65
Hampton Sportswear, 119, 194
Hans Jütte, 175, 194
Harold H. Hoffer & Assoc., 94
Harper, 194
Hawaii Blues, 32, 138
Hawaiian Casuals, 161, 194
Hawaiian Holiday, 12, 194
Hawaiian Incentive Services, 183, 194
Hawaiian Original, 194
Hawaiian Palm, 113, 194
Hawaiian Print, 194
Hawaiian Surf, 194
Hawaiiana, 7
Helen's, 75, 194
Hilo Hattie, 62, 68, 122, 138, 150
Hoaloha, 7, 194
Holiday Sportswear, 20, 194
Honalulu Hawaii, 194
Hookano, 59, 93, 194
Hot Tamales, 184, 194
Howie, 11, 194
HRH, 95, 97, 158, 194
Hukilau Fashions, 14, 194, 195
Hutspah, 195
H.Y.C.T., 195

Iceberg, 195
Impaq Hawaii, 49, 195
Imperial, 90, 195
INC International Concepts, 171, 195
In Gear Fashions, 48
Iolani, 122, 123, 129, 153, 195
Iolani Palace, 17, 23
Island Creations, 27, 195
Island Fashions, 51
Island Fever, 195
Island Fleur, 87
Island Image, 128, 129, 163, 195
Islander, 122, 171, 195

Jade Fashions, 131, 195
Jahaca Prints, 195
Jams World, 195
Jantzen, 28, 29, 30, 95, 96, 129, 159, 195
Japanese Bazaar, 19, 195
Java Wraps, 117, 195
Jayshire, 90, 120, 195
J.J. Cochran, 56, 195
Jockey, 196
Joe Kealuhas, 79, 196

Joe Namath, 95, 196
John Severson, 51
Jolen, 196

K.A.D. Clothing Co., 57, 179, 196
Kahala, 30, 51, 60, 100, 103, 196
Kahana Manufacturing Company, 31, 196
Kahanamoku, 55
Kahili, 64, 196
Kai Nani, 59, 112, 196
Kalaheo, 140, 196
Kamehameha, 5, 6, 17, 18, 19, 30, 120, 158, 196
Kane Malia, 130, 196
Kanoi Koi, 14, 196
Kapito, 196
Ke Nui, 6, 196
Kennington, 196
Keoni of Hawaii, 5, 6, 186
Khaki Safau, 11, 196
Kilii's of Hawaii, 143
Kilohan, 7, 134
King Size, 28, 196
Kings Road, 126, 197
Kishora, 101, 197
Koko Knot, 48, 142
Kole Kole, 26, 112, 197
Koman, 184, 197
Kona Kai, 29, 30, 197
Kramer's, 101, 197
Krazy Klothes, 104, 197
Krush Hawaii, 14, 197
Kulani Beach, 72, 197
Kunakai, 28
Kuonakakai, 20, 197
Kuu Ipo, 7, 197

L.A. Style, 106, 197
Laguna, 109, 197
Lauhala, 147, 197
Leilani, 62, 197
Levi Straus, 168, 197
Le Tigre, 48, 197
Liberty House, 21, 52, 144, 197
Life's A Beach, 197
Linda Bertozzi, 125, 197
Live, 141
Liz Claiborne, 104, 198
Locals Only, 172, 198
Luau Sportswear, 110, 198
Lucky Beach, 40, 45, 62

Mach II, 164, 198
Machin Shirtmaker, 38, 198
MacRoss Creation, 94, 198
Made in Bangledesh, 143
Made in California, 53, 83, 89, 99, 101, 102, 198
Made in Hawaii, 9, 13, 27, 30, 49,

54, 92, 116, 136, 137, 141, 151, 166, 169, 170, 183, 198
Made in Japan, 43, 59, 198
Made in USA, 65, 125
Malibo, 25, 198
Malihini, 21, 42, 48, 150, 198
Mambo, 36, 43, 44, 68, 69, 76, 80, 82, 108, 113, 114, 154, 161, 164, 165, 168, 187, 198
Manhattan, 20, 198
Manonoke, 44
Marc Edwards, 79, 198
Marcdaniels, 12
Margenta, 50, 199
Marjy Stevens, 156, 199
Mark Twain, 153, 199
Marro Bay, 41
Matson Line Navigation Co., 6, 23
McDonald's Restaurant, 182
McGregor, 36, 111, 13, 146, 147, 199
McInerny, 120
M.E. Sport, 178, 199
Meigs, John, 5
Mene's, 149
Men's Store, The, 127, 199
Michael Gerald Ltd., 85
Mignot & Mignot, 94, 199, 203
Mistral, 199
Mitford, 60, 199
Miyamoto, Koichiro, 37
Modesto, 199
Montage Tropics, 74, 199
Monticerutti, 42, 199
Morro Bay, 199
Mr. Kailua, 133
Mukai Fashions, 34, 199
Munsingwear, 135
Musashiya, 37, 38, 110, 199
Mylan, 170, 199

Napili, 70, 199
National, 111, 119, 199
National Shirt Shops, 170
Natural Issue, 97, 200
Nautica, 200
Network, 138
NEWS, 200
Nichole Miller, 184, 200
NLMT, 39, 187, 200

No Boundaries, 200
No Dice, 200
Northwest Orient Airlines, 175
Nui Nalu, 16, 200

Ocean Current, 93, 200
Ocean Pacific, 177
odo, 57, 145, 200
Old Navy, 86, 94, 118, 181, 200
Onita, 200
On the Brink, 2, 200
OP, 68, 200
Orchid Fashions, 10, 200
Original Island Sport, 118, 200
Outrigger Canoe Club, 15, 88

Pacific Isle Creations, 14, 15, 50, 162, 200
Pacific Legend, 104, 200
Palaka, 17
Pali, 89, 155, 200
Palm Bay, 63
Palm Island of Miami, 8, 88
Palm Tree of Banford, 149
Paradise Blue Lagoon, 127, 200
Paradise Found, 40, 95, 140, 145, 151, 163, 200
Paradise Hawaii, 163
Paradise of the Pacific, 117, 200
Paradise Sportwear, 78, 157, 201
Pareu, 132, 133
Paul Smith, 201
Pazzo, 16, 77, 161, 201
Pearl Harbor, 17
Penney's, 19, 29, 111, 112, 131, 201
Pennleigh, 57, 201
Peppermint Bay, 56, 109, 201
Personality, 92, 201
Peter Et Jon, 176, 201
Phat Farm, 8, 39, 40, 43, 111, 201
Pierre Cardin, 130, 201
Pineapple Connection, 56, 85, 118, 180, 201
Pleasant Hawaiian Holidays, 9
Poi Pounder Tog, 83, 201
Polyneisan, 35, 85, 201
Pomaré Tahiti, 136, 144, 201
Presence, 40, 84, 91, 201

Pride, 201

Ralph Lauren, 67, 161
Random Wear, 170, 201
Raycrest, 201
Reef, 141, 201
Regatta, 97
Regular Joe, 107, 201
Repáge, 201
Reyn Spooner, 176, 202
Richard Douglas, 202
Riches, 99, 202
Rittenhouse Collection, 140, 202
R.J.C., 92, 105, 140, 202
Robert Graham, 202
Robert Stock, 181
Robin Hood, 167, 202
Ross Sutherland, 22, 35, 202
Roundy Bay, 86, 202
Route 66, 13, 86, 98, 202
Royal Creations, 132, 202
Royal Hawaiian, 31, 58, 79, 144, 151, 202
Royal Islander, 87, 202
Royal Palm, 101, 172, 202
Rusty, 202

Saginaw, 8, 53, 202
Sandwich Islands, 17
Savage, Eugene, 6, 19
Scorpio, 148, 202, 205
Sea Island, 31, 105, 151, 202, 203
Sears, 28, 29, 33, 126, 127, 137, 143, 203
Sea Valente, 203
Seawanee, 100, 203
Shaheen's, 148, 183, 203
Shore Things, 139, 141, 203
Shoreline Hawaii, 15, 203
Silk Club, 203
Squire of California, 119
SR. Clifford Holiday Wear, 66, 203
Styled for County Road, 203
Substudio, 203
Sun Dek, 133
Sun Fashions, 203
Sun Fashions of Hawaii, 182, 203
Surf In, 203

Surf Line Hawaii, 136, 139, 203
Surf 'N Sand, 21, 157, 203
Surfriders Sportswear, 18, 81, 182, 203

Taboo, 39, 203
Tamaré, 13, 142, 203
Tapa Design, 24-36, 203
Terrace Club, 34, 203
T.H.C. Hawaiian Textiles, 186
Three Sisters, 102, 203
Thums Up For Him, 63, 66, 204
Tina Fashions, 12, 204
Tommy Bahama, 85, 148, 159, 204
Tommy Hilfiger, 136
Topflight, 146, 154, 204
Tori Richard, 146, 149, 204
Towncraft, 29, 177, 204
Trader Joe Stores, 184
Trans-Pacific Textiles, 204
Tribes, 180, 204
Tropical Fashions, 204
Tropicana, 10, 19, 21, 26, 37, 41, 70, 127, 204
Tropicool, 35, 204
Trump, Donald J., 148
Trust, 39, 204

ubc, 130, 204
Ui-Maikai, 8, 11, 12, 32, 132, 143, 173, 204
Union Bay, 116, 204
Utility, 142, 174, 178, 204

Waltah Clarke's, 128, 205
Wardrobe Ltd., The, 100, 205
Watumull's, 22, 52, 205
Wave, 205
Wear to Fish, 105, 205
Weekender Traveler, 96
Westwood Casuals, 73, 205
Wheatley, 205
White Oak, 171
Windswept, 205
Woolrich, 205

Yo Wear, 176, 205

Zoodas, 205

Hula Group

 ## Last Request

Bury me in a Hawaiian shirt.
Aloha.